Louise B. (

The Ridge

MARRIAGE AND DEATH NOTICES

FROM

COLUMBIA, SOUTH CAROLINA, NEWSPAPERS

1792-1839

BY

BRENT H. HOLCOMB, C.A.L.S.

SOUTHERN HISTORICAL PRESS
%The Rev. S. Emmett Lucas, Jr.
P. O. Box 738
Easley, South Carolina 29640

ISBN   0-89308-270-8

INTRODUCTION

The compilation of these marriage and death notices has been one of the most difficult tasks of its kind. These newspapers are scattered from South Carolina to New England. The Columbia files were probably destroyed in the fire of 1865, which left this city in ruins. We are most fortunate that files and issues elsewhere have been preserved.

While the titles of these newspapers vary from time to time, the papers usually were known by a brief title such as Gazette, The Telescope, etc. For the listing of the newspapers and their locations, consult the Contents page. My thanks to the following people for their help in compiling these notices: Ms. Carol Roberson Johnson, Shrewbury, Massachusetts; Mrs. Mary McCampbell Bell, Arlington, Virginia; Mr. Paul Ochenkowski, New Haven, Connecticut.

Other books helpful for searching notices of this time period are Marriage, Death, and Estate Notices from Georgetown, S. C., Newspapers 1791-1861; Marriage and Death Notices from the Charleston Times 1800-1821; Marriage and Death Notices from Camden, S. C., Newspapers 1816-1865; Marriage and Death Notices from the Pendleton (S. C.) Messenger 1807-1851: and Marriage and Death Notices from the Charleston Observer 1827-1845.

Brent H. Holcomb, C. A. L. S.
Columbia, South Carolina
September 16, 1981

CONTENTS

Notices from the South Carolina Gazette   1-24
    papers in the American Antiquarian Society,
    Worcester, Mass. pp. 1-10

    papers in the South Caroliniana Library,
    USC, Columbia, SC   pp. 11-24

    papers in the Library of Congress,
    Washington, D. C.   pp. 25-28

Notices from the Telescope   29-66
    papers in the South Caroliniana Library,
    USC, Columbia, SC   pp. 29-50

    papers at the University of North Carolina,
    Chapel Hill, N. C. pp. 51-53

    papers in the Rock Hill Public Library,
    Rock Hill, S. C.   pp. 53-57

    papers in the Virginia Historical Society,
    Richmond, Virginia pp. 57-66

Notices from the Columbia Hive   67-74
    papers in the South Caroliniana Library,
    USC, Columbia, SC   pp. 67-74

    paper in the Connecticut State Library,
    Hartford, Connecticut   p. 74

Notices from the Southern Times and State Gazette 75-96
    papers in the South Caroliniana Library,
    USC, Columbia, SC pp. 75-82

    papers in the Wessels Library, Newberry
    College, Newberry, SC   pp. 82-96

The following issues are of the <u>South Carolina Gazette</u> and variant titles presently housed in the American Antiquarian Society, Worcester, Massachusetts.

Issue of July 10, 1792

Charleston, June 28. On Monday last was executed, pursuant to his sentence, John Feller, for attempting to pass a note, knowing the same to be forged. He declared his innocence of the crime for which he died, with his latest breath. He died with the greatest fortitude.

Issue of September 15, 1792

Fredericksburg, August 16. On Wednesday evening the 8th instant, Mr. John Brock jun. was murdered near his house in Spotsylvania county. His body was found the next day, lying in the road, with a contusion on the back of his head, and several attempts had been made to cut his throat. Four negroes, the property of his father, have since confessed themselves the actors in this tragic scene and are committed to gaol. He has left a wife and several small children to lament his unhappy end.

Issue of October 6, 1792

Columbia, Oct. 6. Lately died in Philadelphia, Mrs. Smith, consort of the Hon. William Smith, member of Congress from this State.
On Monday last died, near Winnsborough, Mrs. Eliza Winn, wife of John Winn, jun. Esq.

Issue of October 13, 1792

Columbia, Oct. 13. The Earl of Guildford (late Lord North) died in London on the 4th of August last, in the 61st year of his age.
On the same day died, after a few hours illness, Lieutenant-General Burgoyne.

Issue of November 10, 1792

Columbia, Nov. 10. Sir Richard Arkwright died at Cromford, Derbyshire, England in August last. (eulogy)
Saturday last died, greatly lamented, at the saw-mills, Edisto, Colonel Richard Hampton, of the Congaree.

Issue of April 9, 1793

A short time since died, at his plantation on Pedee, greatly lamented, William Wilson, Esquire, a member of the Senate and one of the Justices of the Quorum.

Issue of May 21, 1793

Winchester, April 15. About three weeks ago, Thomas Ross, Postrider, fell a sacrifice to the Indians in the wilderness. Ross had undertaken to come in, accompanied by only two other persons, who when the attack was made, were both wounded. The savages decapitated him, fixes his head upon a stake, left it by the side of the trace, and carried off the mail, which it is said

contained besides the letters, a considerable sum of money.
    Charleston, April 30. Married on Tuesday evening last, Mr.
James Miles of Charleston, to Miss Rachel Porcher, daughter of
Samuel Porcher, Esq. of St. Peter's parish, deceased.

Issue of August 13, 1793

    On Monday the 29th ult. was married at Union Court-house,
Doctor John Conyers, lately from Georgia, to the amiable and
accomplished Mrs. Nancy McKibben, widow of the late John McKibben
of this place.

Issue of April 4, 1794

    Died a few days ago, at Lemington, in this county, Mr. Thomas
Gerald, in his 98th year.

Issue of August 8, 1794

    Married on Saturday last, Mr. James Douglas to Miss Rebecca
Calver, daughter of John Calvert, Esq.

The following issues are found in the Houghton Library, Harvard
University, Cambridge, Massachusetts.

Issue of January 23, 1795

    Died on the night of the 15th inst. after a short illness,
Doctor Henry H. Tillinghast, of this town.

Issue of July 24, 1795

    Died on the 26th ult. at Washington, in the State of Georgia,
Mr. Daniel Terondet. On Monday the 27th, in the town of Augusta,
Mr. Morris Pardue.

Issue of March 11, 1796

    Married, near this town, on the 3d instant, by the Revd. Mr.
Dunlap, Mr. Thomas Heath to Miss Mary Williamson, daughter of
Mr. Rollen Williamson, both of Richland county.
    Died on the 16th ultimo, in 96 district, the honorable Patrick
Calhoun, senator of the election district of Abbeville.

Issue of July 15, 1796

    Died, on Thursday, the 7th instant, at the house of Major
Geiger, on the Congaree, Col. James Beard, aged 63 years.

Issue of July 29, 1796

    Died, on the evening of Friday the 22d instant, at his house,
about 8 miles from this town, Captain Ethiel Heath, a respectable
inhabitant of Richland County.

Issue of August 5, 1796

Died on the 25th ult. at the house of Benjamin Gray, Esq., in
the city of Charleston, Capt. William Benson, one of the judges
of Spartanburgh county, & for many years past a member of the house
of representatives of this state. He has left a widow & thirteen
children to lament the loss of an affectionate husband & tender
father.

Lately, on the Congaree, in Orangeburgh district, Mr. Lewellen
Threewitts.

Issue of September 2, 1796

Died on the 25th ult., at the house of Mr. Smith, near Dor-
chester, on his way home from Charleston, Mr. John Halliday, merchant of this place.

Issue of September 9, 1796

Died on Monday last, after a long & painful illness, which she
bore with much Christian fortitude, Mrs. Mary Hendrick, the amiable
consort of Doctor Robert Hendrick, of this town.

Issue of December 16, 1796

Died at Winnsborough on Sunday the 12th instant, David Evans,
Esquire. (eulogy)

Issue of December 20, 1796

Married on Wed. last, Mr. Peter Witten to the amiable & accomplished Miss Eleanor Hails, both of this county.

Issue of January 6, 1797

Died on Wed. last, after a short illness, Mr. Thomas Patrick.

Issue of January 20, 1797

Died, on Wed. last, Mrs. Catherine Geiger, the amiable consort
of Major Jacob Geiger, of Congaree.

Died, lately at Presque' Isle, Anthony Wayne, commander in
chief of the American army.

Issue of February 17, 1797

Married yesterday, by the Rev. Mr. Dunlap, Mr. William Smart
to Miss Sally McLemore, both of this town.

Issue of March 3, 1797

Died in Richland county, on the 9th ult., at the house of
Col. William Goodwyn, Capt. John Goodwyn. (eulogy).

Issue of March 10, 1797

Married on Thursday the 22d ult., in Fairfield county, Major
Aromanus Liles, to Miss Polly Means, both of that county.

Married on the 23d ult. by the Revd. Mr. O'Farrel, Mr. Thomas
Baldrich of St. Matthews Parish, to the amiable Miss Elizabeth

Howell, 2nd daughter of Robert Howell, of the Congaree.

Issue of April 14, 1797

Married on Sunday last, David R. Evans, Esq., attorney at law to the amiable Miss Peggy Winn, daughter of General Richard Winn, both of Fairfield county.

Issue of June 23, 1797

Married on Wednesday last, by the Rev. Mr. David E. Dunlap, Mr. Thomas Wade of Lancaster county, to the amiable Miss Amy Tillinghast, daughter of Dr. Henry H. Tillinghast, deceased, of this town.

Issue of September 15, 1797

Married on Wed. evening last, Capt. S. Lunsford, to Miss Rebecca Wade, daughter of Capt. George Wade, both of this town.
Died on Wed. last, Mrs. Compty, wife of Major John Compty, of Broad River.

Issue of September 22, 1797

Died, at Savannah, on the 4th inst., Mr. Laird Harris McCaule eldest son of the late Rev. Thomas Harris McCaule--17 years of ag
Died at her father's house, near Columbia, after a short but very severe illness, Miss Harriott Baker, daughter of Mr. J. Baker...only in her eleventh year.... (eulogy).

Issue of September 29, 1797

Died at Camden, on Friday the 22d inst., Dr. James Martin, of that place.

Issue of October 6, 1797

Married on Tuesday the 26th ult., Mr. Christopher Thompson, merchant of this town, to Miss Sophia Harrison, daughter of Burr Harrison, Esq., of Fairfield county.

Issue of November 21, 1797

On Thurs. last, Mr. Alexander Hall of this town was married to Miss Nancy Kincaid, daughter of James Kincaid, Esq.

Issue of April 27, 1798

Died on Monday last, Mrs. Mary Taylor, the amiable consort of Mr. Jesse Taylor, of Richland county.

Issue of April 5, 1799

Died in Charleston, on Tues. the 26th ult., Mr. Jose Daniel, of the Congaree.
Died on Monday last, Mr. William Howell, of Richland county.

Issue of August 30, 1799

Married on Wednesday evening last, Mr. Henry McGowen, to Mrs. Elizabeth Compty, both of this place.
Married in Ninety-six District, on the 26th of July last, Mr. Minyard Harris, to Miss Kittey Hightower.
Died in Granby, on Tuesday evneing last, Mrs. Catharine Johnson, wife of Mr. Samuel Johnson, merchant of that place.

Issue of September 27, 1799

Died on Tuesday evening last, Mr. John Faust, an old inhabitant of Richland county.

Issue of November 29, 1799

We learned from Christ-church parish, that on Saturday evening last, after a general muster of the militia, Messrs. R. Byrd & George Barton remaining alone on the field, a dispute arose between them; and that the former was killed by a load of shot from a gun fired by the latter. Mr. Byrd was a schoolmaster, & has left a wife & three or four children to bewail their loss.
Died at Nassau (N.P.) on the 29th ult. after a short but serious illness, Mr. John Wells, printer, formerly of Charleston.

Issue of June 20, 1800

Married on Wednesday evening last, by the Rev. Mr. Dunlap, Mr. John Wych, to Miss Nancy Williamson, both of this town.

Issue of May 22, 1801

Married on Thursday the 14th instant, William Rees, Esq., of the high hills of Santee, to Miss Elizabeth Adamson, daughter of Mr. John Adamson of Camden.

Issue of May 29, 1801

Married, lately at Carleton, Maryland, by the Right Reverend Bishop Carroll, Miss Carroll, daughter of Chs. Carroll, Esq. of Carleton, to Robert Goodloe Harper, Esq.

Issue of July 10, 1801

Married, a few days since, Col. Wade Hampton, of Richland district, to Miss Polly Cantey, daughter of the late John Cantey, esq., deceased, of Santee.

Issue of August 28, 1801

Died at McCord's Ferry the 18th instant, Mr. John Brown, son of Capt. Richard Brown, of Richland district. He was a worthy honest young man & is much lamented by all who knew him.

Issue of May 20, 1803

Married on Tuesday last, Mr. David Kennerly to Miss Susanna Lyles.
Died on Tuesday evening last, at his residence near this town, Mr. David Fleming.

GAZETTE

Issue of June 3, 1803

Married, on Thursday the 19th May, at Savannah, by the Rev. Mr
Holcombe, Judge Trezevant of this state, to Mrs. Henrietta Morel,
relict of the late honorable John Morel, of Georgia.

Married on Sunday evening last, Mr. Michael Moore, merchant,
to Mrs. Rebecca Lunsford, both of this town.

Died at Philadelphia, half after eleven o'clock, on Monday
the 9th of May, General Stephens Thomson Mason, one of the sena-
tors representative of the state of Virginia, in the Congress of
the U. S.

Issue of August 5, 1803

Died on the 30th day of last month, Mrs. Jane Wilson Rogers,
wife of the Rev. James Rogers, of Fairfield district...in the 25th
year of her age. (eulogy).

Issue of September 2, 1803

Married on Sunday evening last, in the village of Granby, by
the Reverend Mr. Dunlap, Lieut. Peter Lumpkin, to the amiable Miss
Charlotte Caroline Seibels, daughter of Mr. Jacob Seibels, merchar
of this place.

Died at Edgefield Courthouse on Sunday evening, the 21st ult.,
Elizabeth Giles Dozier, only child of Abraham G. Dozier, esquire
of said place, aged 13 mo. & 4 days. (eulogy).

Issue of September 23, 1803

Departed this life on Monday last in the 70th year of his age,
James Foster, preacher of the Gospel. (eulogy).

Issue of October 7, 1803

Washington Sept. 13   Died on the 13th inst., Commodore Barry.
(eulogy).

Issue of October 14, 1803

On Tuesday last departed this life in the 23d year of her age,
Mrs. Nelly Parker, consort of Mr. Thomas Parker, merchant of
Charleston, late of Sheffield, in England. Mr. Parker, who was
married but a few months ago in the city of Baltimore, reached
this place with his family last Monday fortnight, on his way to
Charleston, intending there to fix his permanent residence....

Issue of November 4, 1803

On Tuesday morning, the 1st instant, departed this life, in
the 43d year of his age, Dr. William Montgomery, of this place.
He was a native of Carlisle in Pennsylvania...(eulogy).

Issue of November 29, 1803

Died very suddenly on Sunday night last, Mr. John Calvert,
an old & respectable inhabitant of this place.

Issue of July 15, 1803

Married on Tuesday evening last, by the Rev. Mr. Dunlap, Mr. Robert Clark of Charleston, merchant, to the amiable Miss Sally Tillinghast, of this town.

Issue of January 20, 1804

Married in Baltimore on Saturday the 24th ult., Jerome Bonaparte to Miss Elizabeth Patterson, eldest daughter of Mr. William Patterson, merchant of that city.

Issue of February 3, 1804

Died on the night of the 20th ult. at his plantation on Dutchman's creek, in Fairfield district, Mr. Jonathan Belton, planter & merchant, of a short & painful illness. He has left a disconsolate widow, one son & numerous acquaintances to lament his loss. (eulogy).

Married, at Boston, on the 7th ult., by the Rev. Dr. West, Capt. Peter Geyer, aged 62, to the amiable & accomplished Miss Polly Sancry, aged 17.

Married at Athens (Ver.), Master Silas Chaplain, aged 15, to Miss Susannah Powers, aged 13!!!

Issue of January 27, 1804

Died in the N. parish of Weymouth (Mas.) widow Mary Ripley, who had attained (wanting a few days) the age of 104 years. (eulogy)

Issue of March 9, 1804

Died in England, John Tucker, a soldier in Ashford barracks. He died at 4 o'clock in the morning; before 12 the same day, his widow was married to another man & in the evening, the happy couple followed the corpse of the first husband to the grave as chief morners (sic).

Issue of March 30, 1804

Died lately, at his residence in Richland district, a few miles below Columbia, Dr. Charles William Koester.

Issue of May 15, 1804

Died on the 7th inst., at the late residence of the honorable Commodore Alexander Gillon, Congaree, Beaver Creek, Bernadus Buyck, aged 36, a native of Ghent in Flanders.

Issue of June 8, 1804

On Sunday night, the 27th instant, between the hours of eleven & twelve o'clock, Mr. Richard Johnston, planter, of St. Paul's Parish, hearing a considerable noise among his dogs, adjacent to the house, went out to learn the cause; when he was immiediately shot dead upon the spot, receiving several shot in different parts of his body. The perpetrator of this dead (sic) is supposed to be a fellow belonging to Mr. Johnston, who has absconded for some time past. We are concerned to state that Mr. Johnston has left an effectionate (sic) wife & five children to lament the loss....

On Tuesday the 24th of April, Henry Crymes, of Bath County, State of Virginia, under the influence of delirium, broke his skull with a stone...(account) he lived until Thursday evening following....

Died in Ireland, Roger Byrne, the famous Irish giant. He is said to have died of suffocation, occasioned by an extremity of fat, which stopped the play of his lungs, in the 54th year of his age....London paper.

Died, Mr. Barker, formerly a farmer...(no date given)

Issue of July 20, 1804

Married in Charleston, on the 23d of last month, Capt. Thomas Campbell Cox, one of the Editors of "the Times," to Miss Susan Mason Skrine.

Issue of August 11, 1804

Augusta. On Tuesday the 31st July a duel was fought at Middleton's ferry, on the South Carolina side, between William Appling & John Rowe, both of Columbia County; Mr. Appling received a ball the first fire, about the termination of the hair on his forehead, by which he, in a short time, expired. Mr. Appling has left 3 small children & a number of relatives & friends to deplore the loss of an affectionate friend & valuable member of society.

Issue of August 18, 1804

Died in the city of Charleston, on Friday the 10th instant, much lamented by his friends & acquaintances, after an illness of 8 days, which he bore with Christian fortitude & perfect patience, the Rev. Nicholson Waters, aged 65 years, a minister of the Methodist Episcopal church for near 30 years.

Issue of August 25, 1804

Charleston. With great regret we have to state that one of the most atrocious & premeditated murders was perpetrated in this city yesterday afternoon on the body of Mr. James Shaw, merchant of this city, by a young man named Richard Dennis, jun. (account) We believe Mr. Shaw was about 28 or 30 years of age. He was a native of the state of Maryland, & has resided in this state for about 10 years.

Columbia. Departed this life on the 2d of August, Mrs. Mary Dale, wife of Robert Dale, resident of Chester District, in the 19th year of her age, and left her first child, of about 2 hours old, & an affectionate husband, to lament their loss. (eulogy)

Issue of September 8, 1804

Charleston. Yesterday morning, J. H. Stevens, Esq. coroner for Charleston district, held a jury of inquest on the body of Michael Barrett, Esq. attorney at law, who died on Thursday afternoon, suddenly, on the deck of a schooner bound for Savannah, in which he had taken fit....

Issue of September 15, 1804

Died in this place on the morning of the 10th instant, of a violent bilious fever, Mrs. Susanna Dunlap, the wife of the Rev. David E. Dunlap, aged 30 years. Also, on the evening of the same day, & of the same complaint, the Rev. David E. Dunlap, clerk of the Senate, & one of the trustees of the South-Carolina College, aged 36 years. They were interred in one grave on the day following attended by a general & solemn assemblage of the citizens of this place & of Granby....(eulogy).

Issue of November 3, 1804

Petersburgh, Oct. 16. The recent murder of Ira Lane, who was murdered on the 27th ult. aged 7 years, by David Williams, aged 29, both of the town of Melton & county of Cayuga....(account)

Augusta, 27 Oct. Died in Tattnall county, State of Georgia, the 11th of April last, James Thomas in the 134th year of his age.

Issue of December 1, 1804

Died in Newberry district on Thursday the 22d ult., in the 17th year of his age, Mr. William Henry Long, eldest son of Capt. Benjamin Long of that district.

Issue of December 22, 1804

Married, at Santee, on Thursday the 13th inst., Mr. John C. Schulz, merchant of this place, to Miss Susan Flud Canty.

Issue of December 29, 1804

Married on Tuesday evening last, by the Rev. Mr. Harper, Mr. Robert Yates to Miss Elizabeth Williams, both of this town.

Married on the 20th inst. by Charles Allen, Esq.,Mr. James Caldwell, Preceptor of the Academy adjacent to Laurens village to the accomplished Miss Elizabeth Miller, both of Laurens village.

Married on the 20th inst., Mr. Joseph Manley to Miss Peggy Wilson, daughter of Mr. James Wilson, both of Laurens district.

Issue of January 5, 1805

Died on Tuesday the 20th ultimo, at his residence in Sumter District, Laurence Manning, Esq., Adjutant General of So. Carolina, in the 48th year of his age. (eulogy).

Issue of January 26, 1805

Died on Sunday night last, after a very short illness, Mr. Charles Mulholland, of this town, carpenter.

Issue of February 2, 1805

Washington, Jan. 14. Died, on Friday morning, a representative from No.Carolina. (no name).

Issue of February 9, 1805

Married in Charleston, on Thurs. the 24th ultimo, by the Rev. Mr. Le Mercier, rector of the Roman Catholic Church, Mr. Emmanuel Antonio, to the amiable & accomplished Miss Mary Ann Eleonora Champy.

GAZETTE

Issue of March 2, 1804

Married at the High Hills of Santee, on the 21st instant, Mr. Duke Goodman, merchant of Manchester to Miss Elizabeth C. M'Ginny, of the same place.

Issue of March 23, 1805

Married on Wednesday evening last, Mr. Brutus Howard of this town, to Miss Sarah Goodwyn, daughter of Major Francis Goodwyn, of the Congaree.

Died on Wednesday morning the 20th inst., after a few minutes sickness, Mrs. Ann W. Hoy, wife of Mr. Robert Hoy, aged 35 years.

Issue of April 6, 1805

Married, on the 19th ult., Mr. Charles Compty to Miss Polly Sheppard, both of Broad River.

Married on Wed. last, Major James Adams to the amiable Miss Silvia P. Goodwyn, only daughter of Capt. William Goodwyn.

Issue of April 20, 1805

Died on the 3d day of this instant, Mr. Jacob Bickley, resident in the Dutch fork, near Saluda River, in the 52d year of his age, after a short but painfull illness which he bore with Christian fortitude. His death is much lamented by his family, his friends and acquaintances.

Issue of May 25, 1805

Died at New-York, on the 1st inst., at an advanced age, Hugh Gaire, formerly a respectable printer & bookseller of that city.

Issue of June 1, 1805

Married on Thursday evening last, Mr. Alexander Chisolm, to Miss Susanna Sims, of this town.

Issue of June 29, 1805

Married, at Beaufort, on Thursday last, by the Rev. Mr. Palmer Mr. Robert Means, of Charleston, to Miss Mary Hustson Barnwell, eldest daughter of General John Barnwell, deceased.

Died in Camden, on Friday the 14th inst., Mr. Thomas Dinkins, in the 38th year of his age...(eulogy).

10

The following issues of the South Carolina State Gazette and Columbia Advertiser are in the South Caroliniana Library.

Issue of January 11, 1806

Departed this life on the 26th ultimo, Mr. David Henderson, of Newberry District, for many years a resident of that place... left a widow and several children.

Issue of July 19, 1806

Married in this town on Tuesday evening last, by the Rev. Dr. Maxcy, Mr. Elisha Hammond to Miss Catherine F. Spann.

Issue of October 11, 1806

Died in Charleston on Thursday the 30th ult., Guilliam Aertsen, Esq., Cashier of the State Bank, in the 47th year of his age.
Died at Albany, the Hon. William Patterson, one of the Associate Judges of the Supreme Court of the United States.

Issue of October 25, 1806

Departed this life in Newberry District on Tuesday, the 7th inst., at the house of Major Benjamin Long, Betsey Coate, wife of Capt. Henry Coate...She has left a small daughter and numerous train of friends and relations.

Issue of August 9, 1806

Died a few days since at his residence in Lexington District, Mr. Joseph Williams, formerly a member of the State Legislature.
Died on Saturday last, near this place, Mr. William Tait, a native of Scotland.
Died in this town on Wednesday evening last, after a long illness, Mr. James Madison, a native of Virginia.
Died at his plantation in Edgefield District, S. C., on Monday the 28th July, Mr. Mason Moseley...left aged parents and a young widow...murdered by a Negro...forward information to William Moseley, living at Deer Savannah, Edgefield District, on a road leading from Long Cane to Charleston, 16 miles distant from Augusta.   Augusta paper.

Issue of August 16, 1806

Died on Thursday the 7th inst., at his plantation in Fairfield District, Major Thomas Starke, in the 59th year of his age.

Issue of December 6, 1808

Married in Lexington District, on Sunday evening last, by Rev. Mr. Bernhard, Mr. Abner Blocker, of Edgefield District, to Miss Amelia Kennerly, daughter of Mr. Joseph Kennerly, deceased.

Issue of December 13, 1806

Married on Tuesday last in the fork of the Congaree, by the Rev. Mr. Thigpen, Dr. John Lafargue, late of Charleston, to Miss Ann Wood Hirons.

Died in this place, on the 3d instant, Mr. David Baldwin, tanner and currier, in the 52nd year of his age. He was a native of Newark, New-Jersey.

Issue of January 3, 1807

Marriage at Winnsborough, on the 25th ult.,by the Rev. Mr. Reid, Mr. Edward Pearson, to Miss Rachel Yongue.

Issue of January 17, 1807

Died, in St. Bartholomew's Parish, after his return from Columbia, Major John Smiley, a representative from that parish in the present Legislature.

Issue of February 7, 1807

Married in this town on Thursday evening last, Mr. John Bruce to Mrs. Mary Benson.

Issue of January 13, 1813

Died on the 31st December 1812, in Abbeville District, Mrs. Sarah G. Lipscomb, wife of Mr. John Lipscomb and daughter of Col. Samuel Mays, aged 18 years, 7 months and 5 days; she has left the most kind and affectionate husband, a father, mother, seven brothers and one sister....

Issue of September 17, 1813

Died on Monday night last, after a few days illness, Mrs. Mary Bruce, wife to Mr. John Bruce of this town.

Issue of December 5, 1815

Married in Newberry Village on Sunday evening last, by the Rev. Giles Chapman, Mr. Thomas Pratt, merchant, to Miss Dorothy _____ (torn).

Issue of January 2, 1816

Married on Thursday the 28th ult., by the Rev. Fobert B. Walker, Mr. Alex'r Cabeen to the amiable Miss Mary Ann Patterson, both of Chester District.
Died in Granby on the night of Thursday last, after a few days illness, Mr. James M'Gowen, an old and respectable inhabitant of that village.
Died in Granby on Saturday night last, after a few days illness, Mr. David Kelly, merchant of that place.

Issue of August 5, 1817

Married on Thursday evening, the 10th July, by the Rev. Mr. Mallard, Mr. Donald B. Jones to Miss Mary Elvira Rumph, both of Orangeburgh.
Died at Laurens Court House on the 14th ult.,Mr. Thomas Lewers, formerly of this place.

Issue of October 13, 1818

Married on Tuesday evening last, by the Rev. Mr. Capers,

the Rev. Dr. John Walsh to Miss Ann Schutt, both of Columbia.
    Married on the 22d ult., by the Rev. Thomas Bomar, William
Hunt, Esq., attorney at law of Spartanburgh Village, to the amiable
and accomplished Miss Asenith Daniel of the same district.

Issue of January 27, 1827

    Died at her residence in Fairfield District, on the 8th inst.,
Mrs. Elizabeth Finley, in the 64th year of her age. (eulogy)

Issue of February 3, 1827

    Departed this life on the 10th inst., at Winnsborough, Mrs.
Martha Owen, wife of Capt. T. F. Owen, in the 30th year of her age...
left a husband, three children and numerous relations. Her father,
Wm. Cato, Esq., was a soldier in the Revolution. Her remains
were intereed with a young babe in her arms....
    Died, in this place, on Wednesday evening last, Mr. Benjamin
Duyckinch, formerly the editor of the Augusta Chronicle, in the
53d year of his age, a native of N. Jersey, but has resided in
this state for the last 23 years. (eulogy) AugustaChronicle, 13th
ult.

Issue of February 17, 1827

    Married on the 31st ult., by the Rev'd Alston Gibbes, Julius
G. Huguenin, Esq. of St. Luke's Parish, to Theodocia Octavia,
youngest daughter of the late Theodore Gaillard, Jun., Esq.,of
this City.
    On the 1st inst., by the Right Rev. Bishop Bowen, Edward
Rutledge Laurens, Esq., to Miss Margaret Horry Horry (sic), daughter of Elias L. Horry, Esq., all of this city.
    On the 8th instant, by the Rev. Dr. Gadsden, Dr. James Ramsay,
to Eleanor, daughter of the late Henry Laurens, Esq., all of this
City.   Charleston paper.
    Died at her residence in Abbeville District, on the 20th
ult., Mrs. Susan W. Logan, wife of Dr. John Logan, in the 28th
year of her age...left a husband and two lovely children...member
of the Methodist Church.

Issue of March 3, 1827

    Died in this place, yesterday morning, at an advanced age,
Mr. William Miller, a revolutionary soldier, and a resident near
this place. He belonged to the continental army during the
whole of the war and was in the battle of Fort Moultrie.

Issue of March 10, 1827

    Died on the 6th inst., of Plumonary Consumption, at the resi-
dence of Mr. G. T. Snowden, Mr. James Mollan, eldest son of
Stuart Mollan, Esq. of the city of New-York. (eulogy)

Issue of March 24, 1827

    Married on Wednesday evening last, by the Rev. Benjamin Trade-
well, Mr. William Ancrum of Camden, to Miss Julia Arthur, of this
place.
    On the 15th inst., by the Rev. W. Paulling, Mr. Samuel P.
Corben, to Miss Caroline M. Saylor, both of Lexington district.

Died at her residence in Lexington district, on the 22nd of February,Mrs. Lavinia Taylor, relict of Wm. Taylor.

Issue of April 28, 1827

Died at the residence of Hon. Judge Nott, on the 3d inst., H. D. A. Ward, Esq., aged 26...graduate of Yale College (eulogy)

Issue of May 5, 1827

Married on Thursday evening 26th ult.,by the Rev. Mr. Mallory Mr. Joseph Brevard to Miss Keziah Hopkins.
On the same evening by the Rev. Mr. Folker, Mr. Willis White to Miss Louisa Sheppard.
On the same evening, by the Rev. Mr. Tradewell, Mr. Reuben House to Miss Eliza Dinkins.
On Tuesday morning the 20th ult., by the Rev. Mr. Folker, Mr. James Daniel of Spartanburgh to Mrs. Murdock, of this place.
At Augusta, on Thursday the 19th ult., by the Rev. Mr. Talmage, Mr. Paul Fitzsimons, to Miss Eleanor N. White.
Departed this life on the morning of the 13th inst., at his residence in Union District, Mr. William C. Glenn in the 67th year of his age. Mr. Glenn was a native of Virginia, and emigrat to South Carolina shortly after the close of the Revolution, in which he took an active part...left a widow and eight children.

Issue of May 12, 1827

Died at his residence in New York, on Sunday evening last, in the 73d year of his age, the Hon. Rufus King.
Died, on the 1st of May, Hannah, youngest daughter of John Kennedy, Esq., of Chesterville, S. C. (verse)

Issue of May 19, 1827

Death of John Lofton, a member of the Senior class of South-Carolina College, who perished by drowning on the 12th inst....

Issue of May 26, 1827

Married on Thursday evening the 3d inst.,by the Rev. Patrick Folker, James Jones Esq. of Edgefield to Miss Catharine Creyon of this place.
On Thursday the 10th inst., by Professor Henry, Col. F. H. Elmore of Walterborough, to Miss Harriet C. Taylor, daughter of Gov. Taylor, of this place.
On Tuesday the 15th inst., by the Rev. Benjamin Treadwell, Dr James C. Kennerly, to Miss Catherine B. Smith.
Died in this town on Friday evening the 18th inst., B. S. M'-Namara, M. D., a native of Ireland, aged 63.
In this town on Friday morning, the 18th inst., Mr. Thomas White, formerly of Philadelphia, aged 34...interred in the Episcopal burying ground with military honors by the Republican Light Infantry company, of which he was a member.
In Rowley, Mass., on the 7th inst., Mr. Robert S. Coffin, printer, better known as the "Boston Bard," son of the late Ebenezer Coffin, A. M....

Issue of June 2, 1827

Married in Woodville, Mississippi, on Thursday evening, the
3d ult., by the Rev. James A. Fox, the Hon. William Haile, to
Miss Nancy Ioor, eldest daughter of Maj. Gen. John Ioor.
Died on the 23d April last, near Matanzas, the Hon. Israel
Pickens, late Governor of Alabama.

Issue of June 9, 1827

Died in Georgetown, S. C., on the 19th ultimo, Mrs. Clara
Elizabeth Shackleford, aged 24 years, wife of Francis R. Shackleford.

Issue of June 23, 1827

Death of George Kennedy, Esq., post master of Chesterville,
so. Ca. on the 8th inst., in the 63d year of his age.(eulogy)
Thomas T. Cureton, Esq., late of Newberry district, S. C.,
departed this life at his residence in Covington, Ga., on the
18th May last..born in Laurens, S. C., on 31st May 1784, and from
thence removed to Newberry district...sheriff of Newberry District.
(long eulogy)

Issue of July 7, 1827

Married on Thursday evening, the 5th inst., by the Rev. Mr.
Folker, Mr. Wm. Briggs, formerly of Philadelphia, to Mrs. Lydia
M. Brown, of Rahway, N. J.
Died in this town on the 24th June, Mrs. Jane Marks, wife of
Dr. Elias Marks, aged 39. a native of Boston, in Lincolnshire,
England, and came, an orphan, in early life to this country under
the protection of her only brother (long account and eulogy).

Issue of July 14, 1827

Married in this town on Tuesday evening last, by the Rev. Mr.
Stokes, Mr. Rowland Keenan, to Miss Ann Britt.

Issue of July 21, 1827

Married on Tuesday evening last, by the Rev. Mr. Stokes, Mr.
Charles Brenan, to Miss Eliza Smith.
Died in this place on Sunday morning last, Mrs. Susan Arthur,
wife of Mr. Jesse Arthur in the 51st year of her age.
On Thursday morning last, Mrs. Eliza Snowden.

Issue of July 28, 1827

Married on Monday evening last, by the Rev. Patrick Folker,
Dr. Edward Sill to Miss Caroline M. Greenwood, all of this place.
Died on the 20th inst., Napoleon B., infant son of D. E. &
C. Sweeny, aged 2 years, 10 months and 6 days.
Died on Wednesday the 19th inst., Mrs. Eliza Jane Snowden,
wife of Mr. Gilbert T. Snowden, merchant of this place, aged
20 years and 11 months. (eulogy).

GAZETTE

Issue of August 4, 1827

Married at Winnsborough, by the Rev. Mr. Rennie, the Rev. Richard B. Cater, of Abbeville, to Miss Jemima M., daughter of the Rev. Samuel W. Yongue.

Issue of August 18, 1827

Married on the 25th July 1827, Mr. William Birge to Miss Rebecca Bond, all of Newberry District, S. C.

Died on Wednesday morning last, Mrs. Mary Ann Harris, wife of Dr. Benjamin F. Harris, of this place.

Issue of August 25, 1827

Died in Charleston on the 16th inst., of the Yellow Fever, Mr John Wentworth Black, son of Mr. John Black, merchant of this pla aged 21 years and a few days.

At Brunswick Mineral Springs, on the 5th inst., Col. Joseph Hawkins, Comptroller of the State of North Carolina.

Issue of September 1, 1827

Died on Monday the 20th inst., Mrs. Martha Fullerton Rogers, wife of John Rogers, of Fairfield District, in the 30th year of her age...a native of Pennsylvania, but for 12 years a citizen of South Carolina (eulogy).

Issue of September 8, 1827

Married on Thursday evening the 30th ult., by the Rev. Mr. Folker, Mr. Hart Klapman, Auction and Commission Merchant, to Mrs. Mary Tiller, all of this place.

On Wednesday evening the 5th inst., by the Rev. Mr. Tradewell Mr. James Fenton to Mrs. Eliza Grafton, all of Columbia.

Died on Monday morning last, at the residence of James J. B. White, Esq., on Crane Creek, about 10 miles from this place, Mrs. M'Henry, late of Philadelphia, at an advanced age.

Died on the 2d inst., Mrs. Mary G., wife of Mr. John Gray, in the 24th year of her age...native of Philadelphia, and had reside in our town but a few months. (eulogy).

Issue of September 15, 1827

Died on Friday the 7th instant, at his residence near Winns-borough, in Fairfield District, Col. Jesse Havis, an old and respectable inhabitant of that place, and a revolutionary soldier

On the 28th August last, Mr. Elisha Daniel of Lexington district, in the 51st year of his age.

Departed this life in Charleston, on the 2nd inst.,Mr. Peter Murphy, a native of Ireland, but for many years a respectable citizen of that place. (eulogy).

Issue of September 22, 1827

Died on Saturday the 10th inst., Miss Nancy Parrot, daughter of Mr. Thomas Parrot of this district. (eulogy).

Issue of September 29, 1827

Died on Saturday morning, the 22d inst., William M'Cauley, Esq., merchant, of this place, aged 32 years (eulogy).

Departed this life on Friday, the 21st instant, Mr. Conrad Myers, of Richland district, in the 89th year of his age. He was a Revolutionary soldier....

Issue of October 6, 1827

Married on Thursday 20th ultimo, by the Rev. Mr. Folker, Alexander Herbemont, Esq., to Miss Martha Davis Bay, all of Columbia.

Died in Pendleton on the 16th ultimo, Dr. Henry W. Davis, in the 32d year of his age, formerly of this place.

In Augusta, on the 23d ultimo, Major Freeman Walker, in the 47th year of his age.

Issue of October 13, 1827

Married in Greenville on the 19th August last, by the Rev. Mr. Young, Mr. J. H. Service of Charleston, to Mrs. Martha Williford, of Greenville.

Died at Platt Springs, at the residence of Mr. Nicholas Hane, his newphew Henry Hane, a native of Germany, aged about 26 years....

In Charleston, on the 5th inst., of the Yellow Fever, the Rev. T. C. Henry.

At his seat in Edgefield district, on the 2d instant, Capt. John Ryan, in the 82nd year of his age.

In Abbeville district, a few days since, Major John Bowie, in the 88th year of his age, an active partizan (sic) officer of the revolution.

Issue of October 20, 1827

Married on Tuesday the 9th inst., by the Rev. R. C. Mallory, James L. Clark, Esq., to Mrs. Martha S. Scott.

On Wednesday evening last, by the Rev. P. H. Folker, Colonel Esek H. Maxcy to Miss Elizabeth C. Dinkins.

In Lexington district, on Thursday evening last, by the Rev. Mr. Tradewell, Mr. John I. Rawls of this place, to Miss Ann E. Geiger, of that district.

Issue of November 3, 1827

Married on Sunday evening last, by the Rev. Mr. Folker, Mr. George A. Hillegas, to Mrs. Mary Williamson, all of this town.

Issue of November 10, 1827

Died on the 1st inst., of Pulmonary Consumption, at the residence of Dr. Wells, in Columbia, John W. Robeson, M. D., in the 23d year of his age.

Issue of November 21, 1827

Died at the house of Mr. Jesse H. Goodwyn, near this place, on the night of the 29th ult., Mrs. Mary T. Hopkins, in the 58th year of her age.

At Concord, Cabarras Co., N. C., on the 7th November 1827, Mr. George Yeamans, aged 26 years. He was formerly attached to the New York, Philadelphia & Charleston Circuses....

Issue of November 24, 1827

Died in New-York, on Wednesday evening, 14th inst., Thomas Addis Emmet, Esq., (eulogy).

Issue of November 28, 1827

Died in Raleigh, N. C., on Sunday the 18th inst., in the 73d year of his age, John Haywood, Esq., Public Treasurer of North Carolina, which office he has filled 41 years.

Issue of December 5, 1827

Married on Thursday the 29th ult., by the Rev. Mr. Paulding, Mr. Lewis Felder to Miss Mary C. Wolfe, all of St. Mathew's Paris

Issue of December 8, 1827

Married on Thursday evening last, by the Rev. Mr. Rene, Mr. William H. Taylor, to Miss Mary Hails, all of this place.
Died in this town on Monday morning, 3d inst., Mrs. Eliza A. Hilleary, aged 28 years, consort of Mr. William Hilleary, formerl of New-York.

Issue of December 15, 1827

Died in this district on the 7th instant, William Devlin, Esq., a native of Abbeville district, So. Carolina.

Issue of December 22, 1827

Died, on Tuesday afternoon, last, Gen. Jacob J. Faust, of this town. (eulogy).

Issue of December 29, 1827

Married on Sunday evening last, by the Rev. Mr. Reney, Mr. Thomas Waul to Miss Jane E. Dudley.

Issue of January 5, 1828

Married on Thursday evening,December 20th, by the Rev. Mr. Folker, Mr. Robert W. Gibbes, of Charleston, to Miss Caroline Elizabeth, eldest daughter of James S. Guignard, Esq. of this place.
Died in Fairfield district, on the 27th November last, in the 24th year of her age, Mrs. Eliza Jane Taylor, consort of Capt. Samuel S. Taylor. (eulogy)
Died on Sunday, December 23d, of Typhus Fever, Mr. James C. Keith, Student of the South Carolina College. (eulogy).

Issue of January 19, 1828

Married on Thursday evening, the 3d inst.,by the Rev. Mr. Reney, Mr. Samuel Ewart, of this place, to Miss Louisa Hannah Laval, of Charleston.

18

Died in Wintonburg, Conn., on the 16th December, Mr. Adin Lawrence Loomis, in the 32nd year of his age.

Mrs. Sarah Cannon, consort of Col. Samuel Cannon, Sheriff of Newberry district, departed this life on the 15th of November 1827. She was born on the 17th of April 1778, and was brought up in the district where she died. (long eulogy).

Issue of February 9, 1828

Died in this town on Saturday last, Mr. Christopher Barrillon, in the 64th year of his age, a native of Parish, France, and for many years a resident of this place.

Departed this life on Sunday 20th January, Mr. Gneuman Tidwell, of this place, in his 32nd year. (eulogy).

Issue of February 16, 1828

Henry Gardner died in this city, 10th ult., aged 93 years, 5 months and 20 days, born in North Kingston, Rhode Island, 20 July 1734 (account and eulogy).   Charleston Courier, 6th inst.

Issue of February 23, 1828

Married on Wednesday evening last, by the Rev'd Mr. Peixotta, Mr. M. C. Mordecai of Charleston, to Isabella, daughter of Mr. Isaac Lyons, of this place.

On Thursday evening last, by the Rev'd Robert Adams, Captain H. Macon of Sumterville, to Miss Eliza D. Russell, of this place.

On Thursday the 31st January, by the Rev'd Robert Adams, Mr. James E. Williamson, of Richland, to Miss Eliza Ann Kennerly, of Lexington.

Issue of March 15, 1828

Died in Charleston, on the 4th instant, General John Geddes, formerly Gov. of this State, and General of the 4th Brigade of South Carolina Militia. His eldest son, John Geddes Jun., died also on the same day....

At his residence in Alabama, Dallas county, Mr. John C. Smith, in the 35th year of his age. He was born in South Carolina, but for many years a resident of Alabama...left wife and two children.

Issue of April 5, 1828

Married in Lexington district, on Thursday evening last, by the Rev. Mr. Folker, Mr. B. D. Plant, Bookseller, of this town, to Miss Maria, daughter of George Kaigler, of Lexington.

In Fairfield district, on Tuesday evening the 25th of March last, by the Rev. William Holmes, Trezvant De Graffenried, M. D., to Miss Rebecca C. Hill.

In Lexington District on Thursday evening, the 27th of March last, by the Rev. Mr. Kennedy, Mr. William Beard of this town, to Miss Mary Daniel, of Lexington.

On Thursday evening last, by the Rev. Mr. Tradewell, Mr. Edward Harris, to Miss Mary Lovely, all of this town.

GAZETTE

Issue of April 19, 1828

Died in Washington, Geo., Mr. John K. M. Charlton, late edito of the Washington News.

Issue of May 3, 1828

Died on Tuesday the 29th ult., at Sandy River, Chester Distri Mr. William Hall, a native of Scotland. His remains were brough to this place and interred in the Presbyterian burying ground.

Died on the 24th March last, at Stonesville, Greenville dis- trict, Master Josiah Kilgore, son of Josiah Kilgore, Esq. of tha place, in the tenth year of his age (verse).

Issue of May 10, 1828

Died at the residence of Mr. Zeigler, in Orangeburgh district on Friday the 2d inst., Mrs. Ann C. Ripley, consort of Mr. L. Ripley of this town, aged 39 years. Her death was occasioned by a fall received on the 27th ultimo, in leaping from the stage, the horses having taken fright....

In this City, at a quarter before 6 o'clock last evening, the Hon. Thomas Tudor Tucker, Treasurer of the United States, in the 84th year of his age...(eulogy). Nat. Int. 3d inst.

Issue of May 17, 1828

Married on Sunday evening the 4th inst., by the Rev. Mr. McKennis, Mr. Augustus McNeal of this town, to Mrs. Mary Carr of Chester dist.

Died at the residence of John D. Brown, Esq., in this distric on Monday evening last, Delanore B. Pasmore, aged 1 year and 6 months.

Issue of May 24, 1828

Died in this town on Thursday evening last, Mr. R. A. Taylor, formerly of Charleston.

At her fathers residence, Richland District, the 14th inst., Mrs. Caroline Anne Brevard, wife of Theodorus W. Brevard, and daughter of James and Keziah Hopkins, aged 21 years.

Issue of June 7, 1828

Married in Camden on Tuesday evening the 20th ult., by the Rev. Mr. Davis, Mr. Algernon S. Clifton, of this town to Miss Caledonia C. Macoll, of the former place.

Departed this life on the 19th instant, at the residence of Major Allen Jones Green, near Sandford, Dr. James T. Leckie, in his 22d year. (eulogy).

Issue of June 21, 1828

Died in this town, on Monday morning last, Mrs. Mary C. Park, consort of Dr. Thomas Park, in the 54th year of her age.

On the 10th inst., at his residence in Richland district, Captain William Taylor. He was an active partizan in favour of our Independence, during the Revolutionary War with Great Britian aged seventy-one years.

Issue of July 4, 1828

Died on Sunday morning at Malyern, near Stateburg, the Hon. Thomas Waties, one of the Associate Judges of this State. We believe this gentleman as to seniority in office, was the oldest public servant in South-Carolina.

At his residence in Fairfield district, on the 1st inst., Mr. Thomas Muse, in the 83rd year of his age.

At the residence of his mother, in Virginia, Mr. Thomas A. Ponsonby, of the firm of Kyle and Ponsonby of Norfolk, and formerly of this place, in the 21st year of his age.

Issue of July 12, 1828

Married in this town on Thursday evening, the 10th inst., by the Rev. Mr. Folker, Mr. Simeon Wheeler, to Miss Rebecca Hennon, all of Columbia.

Issue of July 19, 1828

Married in Monticello, Geo., on the 19th ultimo, Mr. Asa T. Smith, to Mrs. Mary Ann Yeaman, both of the La Fayette circus, and formerly of New York.

Died in Charleston, on Thursday the 10th inst., Dr. John Ramsay, late a member of the Senate of South Carolina, from St. Paul's Parish.

Issue of July 26, 1828

Died at the Lightwood-Knot Springs, on Tuesday morning last, Harriet Louisa, infant daughter of Mr. Jesse DeBruhl.

Issue of August 2, 1828

Married on Thursday evening last, Mr. David W. Sims, proprietor of the Columbia Telescope, to Miss Ann McGowen, both of this town.

On the same sevening, by the Rev. Mr. Raney, Mr. F. W. Green, to Miss Sarah, daughter of Mr. William Briggs, all of this place.

Issue of September 13, 1828

Died at the residence of his father in this district, on the 19th ult., Thos Heath Jr., in the 27th year of his age.

In Laurens district, on the 13th ult., Mr. Wm. Coleman, and on the 15th Mrs. Coleman, consort of Wm. Coleman, of a short but painful illness. They were taken ill within three hours of each other and died within thirty six.

At his residence in Fairfield district, on Monday the 1st inst., Thomas Means, Esq., in the 62nd year of his age.

Issue of September 20, 1828

Died in Augusta on the 15th inst., Mr. John Thurman, printer, aged 35 years.

On the 23d ult. in Staunton, Va., the Rev. Enoch George, one of the Bishops of the Methodist Episcopal Church, aged about 60 years.

21

Issue of September 27, 1828

Married on the 9th inst., in Morristown, New Jersey, by the Rev. Albert Barns, Mr. James Burnet, Merchant of this town, to Miss Catharine Ann Schenk, of the former place.

Died at his residence in St. Mathew's parish, on the 10th inst., John Reid, Esq., formerly a resident in this town, and for several years a very respectable Tutor in the South Carolina Coll

Issue of October 4, 1828

Married in Frederick county, Virginia, on Thursday the 11th ultimo, by the Rev. Mr. Buck, Mr. Felix Meetze, merchant, of this town, to Miss Jane Bourne, of the former place.

Died in this town on Friday, the 12th ult., Mr. Benjamin Mason, in the 55th year of his age.

At sea, Benjamin W. Booth, Esq., Commander of the United Stat Sloop of War, Lexington.

Issue of October 18, 1828

Died at his residence in Richland district, on the morning of the 29th September last, Jacob Deleon, Esq., in the 64 year of hi age.

At his residence on Little River, on Friday the 10th instant, at an advanced age, Mr. Anthony Pullig, for many years a respectable inhabitant of this district. Mr. Pullig was a native of Prussia, and in his youth, served a considerable time as a horseman in the wars of Frederick the great.

Issue of October 25, 1828

Died of a consumption on Monday the 20th instant, Mr. Samuel Wilson, in the 26th year of his age. Mr. Wilson was a native of Castle Douglass, Scotland, but for the last nine years has been a resident of this place... He was a member of the Republican Light Infantry Company, and the Franklin Debating Club....remains rest in the Presbyterian Church Yrad.

In this town on Tuesday the 21st instant, William Preston, infant son of Mr. John D. Moore, aged 8 months.

On Monday the 20th instant, at his residence in Fairfield, in the 63d year of his age, Robert Milling, Esq., a native of Ireland, but for many years a citizen of this State.

Death of Capt. Robert Henley, of the U. S. Navy, commandant of the Naval Station at Charleston (S. C.), for many years and until recently, an esteemed resident of this Borough, and one of the most distinguished of our naval heroes in the last war with England.... died at his residence on Sullivan's Island, aged 45 years. Norfolk Beacon.

Issue of November 1, 1828

Died in Newberry District, on Friday the 17th ultimo, Mr. Noah Simpson Harmon, son of Mr. John Harmon, in the 21st year of his age.

Issue of November 15, 1828

Died on the 1st instant, Mrs. Deborah Anne Yarborough, wife of Mr. Washington Yarborough, of Fairfield district, aged about twenty years....left an aged mother, brothers, sisters a husband and an infant....

Issue of November 22, 1828

Died at his residence in this place on the 10th instant, Mr. William Briggs, a native of Philadelphia, but for some years past an inhabitant of this town.

On the 15th instant, at his residence in Marion district, Enos Tart, Esq., in the 50th year of his age. Mr. Tart was formally (sic) a member of the Senate, and at the time of his death, Clerk of the Court of Sessions and Common Pleas for that district.

Issue of December 6, 1828

Died at his residence on the 27th ult., Harmon Kinsler, Esq., a citizen of Richland district, aged about 64 years. (eulogy).

Issue of December 13, 1828

Died in this place,on Wednesay the 3d inst., Mrs. Susan M. Brickell, wife of William A. Brickell, Esq. (verse).

Issue of December 27, 1828

Died suddenly on Sunday the 14th inst., Daniel D. White, aged 8 years, 6 months, eldest son of James J. B. White, Esq. of Richland district.

The following issues are on microfilm (N3741) at Perkins Library, Duke University, Durham, North Carolina.

Issue of April 30, 1825

Married on Thursday the 21st instant, by the Rev. Mr. Marcher, Mr. Solomon Huggins to Miss Elizabeth Troublefield, all of this district.

Issue of February 28, 1829

Married in this place on Thursday evening last, by the Rev. Mr. Rennie, Mr. Neal M'Lean, to Miss Mary Briggs, daughter of William Briggs, deceased.

On the 12th inst., by the Rev. Mr. Campbell, the Hon. John Carter, Representative in Congress from South Carolina, to Miss Ellen Marbury, daughter of Captain William Marbury, of Georgetown D. C.

Died at Montpelier, Va., the residence of James Madison, departed this life on Wednesday, February 11, Mrs. Eleanor Madison, the venerated parent of our Ex-president...aged 98 years.

Issue of June 20, 1829

Died on Sunday evening last, Mrs. Eliza Saunders Guignard,

in the 36th year of her age, wife of James S. Guignard, Esqr.,
of this place.
In this place on the 6th instant, Mr. Isaac Frazier, in his
60th year, an old inhabitant of this town.
In Charleston, on the 15th instant, Col. Wm. Rouse, of that
city, in the 74th year of his age.
At the residence of his son, in Roxbury, Mass. on the 7th
inst., Major General Henry Dearborn, aged 78 years and three
months.
At Hamilton, Ohio, on the 19th ultimo, Capt. John Cleves
Symmes, the enthusiastic advocate of the theory of Open Poles and
Concentric Spheres.

The following issues are located in the Library of Congress,
Washington, D. C.

Issue of July 23, 1816

Married, by George Robison, Esq. on Thursday the 27th ult.,
Mr. William Champlain, to Miss Sarah Woodward, all of Fairfield.
In Newberry district, on the 8th of July, Mr. John Bundrick,
to the amiable Miss Elizabeth Odum.

Issue of August 25, 1818

Died, at his residence, in Chester district, S. C., upon
Sunday morning, 9th August, in the 83d year of his age, James
Gore, an old respectable citizen of said district for many years.
He came to his death accidentally; upon Saturday he started to go
to mill with a few bushels wheat, in a little four-wheel carriage
and a negro boy with him: on his way, the horse took a fright
and ran away with the carriage; the old gentleman was thrown out;
had several of his bones broken, and all bruised in a horrid manner
to behold. He lived a few hours after, but never spoke a word
that could be understood. He has left a wife and several children
and grandchildren, and a number of relatives....
In Fairfield district, on the 18th inst., after a long and
painful illness, which she bore with a fortitude more than human,
Mrs. Margaret Montgomery, consort of Mr. Charles Montgomery, sen.
in the 66th year of her age. (eulogy).
On Monday the 17th inst., Mr. Samuel Scott, at his residence
in this district.
On Saturday morning last, after a long illness, Mrs. Sarah
Bremar, widow of Mr. Peter Bremar, deceased.

Issue of March 30, 1819

Married, in the neighborhood, of Stateburgh, on Wednesday
night, the 17th of March, by the Rev. John M. Roberts, Mr.
Halloway James, to Miss R. Howard, daughter of Mrs. Ann Howard,
all of the same neighbourhood.

Issue of April 6, 1819

Married on Thursday evening last, Mr. Henry G. Smith, merchant
of this place, to Miss Peggy Ellison, of York district.

GAZETTE

Issue of April 20, 1819

Married on Thursday evening last, by the Rev. Mr. Hanckle,
Mr. William Mayrant, of Sumter district, to Miss Sarah H. H.
Bay, of this place.

Issue of May 4, 1819

Married in Charleston, on Sunday evening the 25th ult., by the
Rev. Dr. Furman, Mr. David Ewart, of this place, to Miss Madaline
Barns, of that city.
In Baldwin county, Georgia, on Thursday the 22d ult., Mr.
Hiram B. Troutman, formerly at student of the South-Carolina College, to Miss _____ Ellis.
On the 18th of February last, Capt. Joel Spencer, of the U.
States army, to Miss Mary Boatner, of the Mississippi.
In Franklin county, N. C. on Thursday the 13th ult., by the
Rev. Wm. Jones, Gen. Calvin Jones, of Raleigh, to Mrs. Temperance
Jones, widow of Dr. Jones, and daughter of Maj. Wm. Williams, of
Franklin.

Issue of May 25, 1819

Died on Thursday morning last, in the 70th year of her age,
after a long illness, which she bor with Christian meekness and
resignation, Mrs. Ann Waring, widow of the late Benjamin Waring,
Esq.

Issue of June 15, 1819

Married in Fairfield district, on Sunday evening, 6th inst.,
by Thomas T. Williamson, Esq., Mr. Lewis Farmir, to Miss Martha
Boyles, both of that district.

Issue of June 22, 1819

Married on Sunday evening the 12th inst., by the Rev. Mr.
Dunwoody, Mr. John Adams, to Miss Sarah Ware, all of this place.
On Tuesday evening last, by the Rev. Mr. Clifton, the Rev.
Mr. Samuel Dunwoody, of Camden, to Miss Elizabeth H. Harrison, of
this place.

Issue of June 29, 1819

Married on the 16th inst., by the Rev. Darling Peoples, Mr.
John Wolfe Hane, of Granby, to Miss Sarah Tarrant, daughter of
the Rev. Benjamin Tarrant, of Barnwell district.

Issue of July 6, 1819

Married in Newholland, on Sunday evening the 22d ult., Mr.
S. C. Tambaugh, editor of the Free Press, to Miss Ann Wielder,
of Lancaster.
On Thursday the 22d ult., Mr. Peter Hardt, editor of the York
Recorder, to Miss Catharine Sides, of Hanover.
Died, in Augusta, Rackaline Paccotti, aged two months and
26 days. This child was conceived in Italy and born in Africa,
has been to the Havanna and Savannah, and died in Augusta 28th
May 1819.

25

Issue of July 13, 1819

Died in this place on the night of Sunday the 4th inst., after several months illness, Mrs. Mary Stark, wife of Robert Stark, Esq.

On Saturday last, after a long illness, Mr. Wm. Smart, of this distirct.

Issue of July 20, 1819

Departed this transitory existence in Fairfield district, on the 8th inst., Mrs. Jane Porter, in the 56th year of her age. Her death was occasioned by a wound inflicted by a rabid animal. (eulogy and verse).

Died, yesterday morning, after a hew hours illness, occasioned by a bleeding at the lungs, Mr. Robert Delahunt, in the 58th year of his age, a native of Ireland, and for a number of years an inhabitant of this place.

Issue of July 27, 1819

Married on Thursday evening last, by the Rev. Mr. Todd, Mr. Joseph Evans, of this place, to Miss Ann Lyles, of East Granby.

Issue of August 3, 1819

Married on Thursday evening last, by the Rev. Mr. Scott, the honorable Robert Clendinen, of Yorkville, to Miss Mary Myers, daughter of Col. David Myers, of Richland district.

Issue of August 17, 1819

Married on Wednesday evening last, by the Rev. Dr. Walsh, Mr. Samuel Taylor, to Mrs. Sarah Trap, both of this place.

On Tuesday the 3d instant, two negro men, two mules and a horse, were at the same time struck dead by Lightening, at a mill on Broad River, about twenty miles above Columbia. One of the negroes belonged to Mr. George Lightner, and the other to Mr. Freshley, the owner of the mill.

Issue of August 24, 1819

Died on Wednesday night last, Mrs. Rebecca Veal, the wife of Mr. John Veal, of this place.

At the sea shore, near Georgetown, S. C., on the morning of Wednesday the 11th inst., Capt. Joseph Pyatt.

Issue of September 7, 1819

Died on the 2d inst., in this district, Mrs. Margaret Evans, consort of Mr. Richard Evans, in the 25th year of her age.... (eulogy).

At Chesterville, on Sunday the 29th August, after a painful illness, Miss Mary S. Kennedy, eldest daughter of George Kennedy, Esq.

Mrs. Amelia Blocker, wife of Col. Abner Blocker, breathed her last on the morning of the 28th ult...born 23d Feb 1789, and although she had had seven children, yet left but three of very tender years....(eulogy).

Issue of September 14, 1819

Died in Orangeburg District, on the 25th ult., after an illness of five days, of the country fever, Mr. Hezekiah Hotchkiss, Jun. aged 30, a native of New-Haven, Connecticut. He has left a family and numberous friends to lament his early exit.

In Charleston, on the 1st instant, after a few days illness, Col. Keating Lewis Simons, a member of the house of representatives of this state from Charleston district.

at Princeton, N. J. on Saturday the 21st ultimo, the Rev. Samuel Stanhope Smith, D. D. LLD., late President of Princeton College.

Issue of September 21, 1819

Married in Lexington district, on Thursday evening last, by the Rev. Mr. Clifton, Mr. Drury Davis, to Miss Rachel C. Kennerly, both of that district.

On Saturday evening last, by the Rev. Mr. Hankle, Monsieur Francis Dallot, to Mademoiselle Marie A. Chenault, natives of France, and for some time residents of this place.

Departed this life, at Philadelphia, on Wednesday the first instant, General John Rutledge, of Charleston, in this state, in the 54th year of his age.

Departed this life on the 13th inst., Mrs. Mary Rou, aged 36 years, late consort of Capt. George D. Roul, after a severe illness of thirteen days, which she bore with christian fortitude. She has left a tender husband and six children to lament her loss.

Issue of September 28, 1819

Died on Friday the 17th inst., in Charleston,the Rev. Henry Thomas Fitzgerald, one of the Methodist Preachers stationed in Charleston, for the present year. This amiable young man...was a native of N. C.-- at the close of the year 1817, he was recommended by the Wilmington Quarterly Conference, to the Southern Annual Conference; and by them appointed to labour in the Little River Circuit, in the State of Georgia...(eulogy).

On Sunday the 1st of August, at her residence in Chester district, S. C., Sandy River, Mrs. Elizabeth Walker, aged about 72 years. She was twice married, was the mother of twelve children, viz: nine to the first husband and three to the last, with a great increase viz. 57 grandchildren, twenty great grand children. (eulogy)

On the 29th ult., at St. Francesville, Louisiana, aged 23 years, Joshua, the eldest son of Mr. Thomas Beard, of this place, who for the last sixteen or seventeen months was a resident of that place.

Died on the 17th of August, at the residence of David Coalter, Esq., near St. Louis Missouri, in the 42nd year of his age, Edward Darell Smith, M. D., Professor of Chemistry and Mineralogy in the South-Carolina College. (eulogy)

Issue of October 5, 1819

Mr. Thomas Lowry departed this life on the evening of the 9th ult. at his brother's residence, the Rev. James Lowry, in the vicinity of Robertville, Beaufort district... He was the seventh and youngest son of Mr. Wm. Lowry dec. of Fairfield district. (eulogy).

GAZETTE

On Tuesday the 21st of Sept. at the residence of Mr. James
Richardson, in Sumpter district, near Santee river, in the
thirtieth year of his age, Dr. William F. Bradbury, a native of
Portland, in Massachusetts. Dr. Bradbury was regularly initiated
into the practice of Physic, and served with reputation as a
Physician and Surgeon in the army and navy of the United States.
(eulogy).

Departed this transitory life in Fairfield district, after an
illness of ten days, Mr. Austin R. Wright, late a resident of this
town, in the 23d year of his age...left an aged, infirm mother....

The _Telescope_ began publication on December 19, 1815, and
ran for over twenty years, the title varying slightly: The _Tele-
scope_, The _Columbia Telescope_, The _Columbia Telescope and Southern
Political and Literary Register_, etc. The holdings of the South
Caroliniana Library appear first, with other libraries following.
Any duplication of issues of the South Caroliniana holdings are
omitted.

Issue of December 19, 1815

Married in Columbia a few days ago, Col. Abraham Blanding, of
Camden, to Miss Caroline Desaussure, daughter of the Hon. Judge
Desaussure.
  Died in Columbia, on Sunday last, Col. Huggins, senator from
Georgetown.
  A few days ago, by being thrown from a gig, Doctor Finch, of
Newberry.
  In this vicinity, Col. Francis De la Mar, formerly surveyor-
general.

Issue of December 25, 1815

  Married in Centerville, on the 5th inst., by the Rev'd George
Vandever, Daniel H. Tillinghast, Esquire, Attorney at Law, to
Miss Francis W. Earle, daughter of the Hon. Elias Earle.
  Died, in Columbia, on Friday last, Mr. John P. Moore, a Student
in the South Carolina College.
  Near this place, a few days since, Mr. Charles Evans of this
District.

Issue of January 2, 1816

  Died lately in Newberry District, John Henderson, Esq., late
a representative of that District in the State Legislature.

Issue of January 9, 1816

  Died, in this place, a few days, ago, Mr. Peter L. Delane.
Died lately in the 49th year of his age, Dr. Benjamin Smith Barton,
Professor of the Theory and Practice of Medicine and of Natural
History and Botony (sic) at the University of Pennsylvania.

Issue of January 16, 1816

  Died in Columbia, on Sunday last, Mrs. Martha Wade, wife of
Mr. Geo. Wade, an old and respectable inhabitant of this place.
  On the same day, Mrs. Caldwell, the wife of John Caldwell,
  Esq., cashier of the Bank in this place
At Atkaspas, Louisiana, Col. Thomas Gales, Indian Agent, formerly
of North-Carolina.

Issue of January 23, 1816

  Died in Columbia on Saturday evening last, after a very short
illness, Miss Caroline A. Frazer, daughter of the late Dr. James
Frazer.
  On Saturday last, Master Isaac M'Pherson, a Student in College,
son of Gen. Isaac M'Pherson.

TELESCOPE

Issue of January 23, 1816 (contd).

In England, T. Evans and W. Middlemore, Esquires, bankers at
Nottingham.
In Spain, the Lady of General Porlier, lately executed for
Treason.
In London, John Coakley Lettsom, Dr. of Laws, Fellow in the
Royal Society.

Issue of January 30, 1816

Married in Camden, a few days since, Col. Francis A. Delesse
line, of Georgetown, to Miss Amelia Adamson, daughter of Mr. Jol
Adamson.
In Raleigh, on the 16th inst., Lieut. John Carney, late of
U. S. Army, to Miss Ann Lucas, sister to the Editor of the "Rale
Minerva."
Died, yesterday morning, about 8 o'clock, Mrs. Ann Casey, wi
of James Casey, of West Granby.
Died, in Granby, on Sunday week, Mr. Wm. H. Furney, Taylor,
of that place.
Lately, at his residence in Clarendon, Capt. J. Conyers, a
member of the State Legislature from that place.

Issue of February 6, 1816

Died in this town on Monday the 29th ult., Mr. John Taylor,
son of the late Mr. John Taylor.
On Tuesday morning last, Miss Jane Drenon, after a short ill
ness.
On Saturday night last, Mr. William Marshall, of the firm of
Marshall and Russell.

Issue of February 13, 1816

Died in Granby on the 2d inst., Mr. Jesse Coryell, of that
place.
In Edgefield District, on the 30th ult., General Samuel Mays
formerly a member of the State Legislature.
Very Suddenly, on the 18th of January, at Bedford, Va., Majo
John Reid, of the U. S. Mary, the well-known aid of Gen. Jackson
during the late war.

Issue of February 20, 1816

Married in this place, on the 8th inst., Mr. David Bryant,
of Georgia, to Miss Catharine Holmes.
In Lexington District, on Thursday evening last, Mr. Jacob
Kougler, to Miss Penelope Johnston.

Issue of February 27, 1816

Married in Fairfield District, on the 22d inst., by Rev. Mr.
Rogers, Dr. Alexander Wylie, to Miss Mary Ann Pearson, both of
that district.
Died, in this town on Thursday week, Mr. Rich'd M'Gee.
On Saturday, 17th inst., at his residence in this district, Mr.
William M'Ilwain.
At his residence on Saluda River, on Wednesday, the 13th ins
Col. Joel Abney, a very worthy citizen of Edgefield District.

30

Issue of March 5, 1816

Died of the prevailing Epidemic, in Cambridge, Abbeville District, on the 23d ultimo, Abram Giles Dozier, Esquire, in the 42d year of his age...spent 17 years of his life in the practice of law. (long eulogy)

Issue of March 12, 1816

Married in Camden, on the 29th ult., by the Rev. Mr. Reid, Mr. David Schrock to Miss Ann V. Cantey.

In Greenville, Dr. Richard Harrison, to Miss Maria S. Thompson, daughter of the Hon. Judge Thompson.

Issue of March 19, 1816

Married in Fairfield district, on the 3d inst., Mr. Edmund Fair to Miss Esther Chapman.

Died in St. Matthew's Parish, on the 5th inst., Capt. Robert Hails.

In this place, on Thursday last, Mr. Warren Patterson, chairmaker.

Issue of March 26, 1816

Died in St. Matthews parish, on the 4th inst., the Rev. Mr. James O'Farrell, in the 62d year of his age.

Issue of April 2, 1816

Married on Friday the 10th ult., by Wm. Pearson, Esq., Mr. William Thornton, to Miss Mary Matthews.

On Tuesday the 12th, Mr. John Nelson to Miss Susannah Ethridge. On Thursday the 14th, Mr. Andrew Mickler, to Miss Rachel Stanton.

Issue of April 9, 1816

Departed this life at his residence in Lexington District, on the 26th of March, Mr. Mathias Wessinger. (eulogy)

Issue of April 16, 1816

Married in Granby, on the 11th instant, by the Rev. Dr. Montgomery, Mr. John Parr, of this place, to Miss Mary Saylor, of Lexington District.

In Newberry, on the 7th inst.,by the Rev. Giles Chapman, Doctor Thomas Shell to Miss Precious Shoppert.

Issue of April 23, 1816

Died at his lodging in Georgetown, D. C., the Hon. Richard Stanford, a Representative in Congress from North Carolina, aged about 47 years...a representative for nearly twenty years, and was the oldest member of the House. Nat. Int.

In Fredericksburg, Va., the 31st March, in the 72d year of his age, the venerable Francis Asbury, Bishop of the Methodist Episcopal Church.

Issue of May 14, 1816

Married in Camden, on the 2d inst., by the Rev. Mr. I. Smith, Mr. Elias Ford to Mrs. Rebecca Burchmore.

Died, on Saturday week, in Fairfield District, at the residen of Philip Pearson, Esq., Doctor Alexander Wylie. (eulogy)

Issue of May 21, 1816

Married in the village of Newberry, on the 9th inst., Dr. Jam Shell to Miss Rebecca H. Berry, both of that place.

Died at Athens, New York, suddenly, the Hon. Samuel Dexter, of the State of Massachusetts.

Issue of May 28, 1816

Died on Tuesday evening, the 7th instant, Mr. Jeremiah Shanno of Orangeburgh District,in the 18th year of his age.

On the 17th of last month, Mrs. Nancy Hannah, wife of James Hannah, post-master of the Huntingdon post office.

Married in this town on Thursday evening last, Mr. John Yance to Mrs. Ann W. Delane.

Issue of June 4, 1816

Died at Laurel Hill, N.C.,on Sunday May 2d, Mrs. Mary McFarla consort of Duncan McFarland, Esq.

Issue of June 11, 1816

Died on Sunday night last, Wright C. Ryson, Esq., Sheriff of Richland District.

In Edgefield District, a few days ago, Mrs. Marsh (murdered).

Issue of June 25, 1816

Married on Thursday last, Capt. Benj. Waring to Miss Martha Goodwin.

On Sunday last, Mr. Thomas Hutchinson to Miss Mary Boatright. On the 6th inst., Robert R. Pearson, Esq., of Fairfield, to Miss Hannah S. Henderson of Newberry District.

Died at the Creek Agency, on the 6th inst., Col. Benjamin Hawkins, Agent for Indian Affairs. He was one of the Revolutiona patriots...(eulogy) Georgia Journal.

Issue of September 3, 1816

Died in Putnam County, Georgia, a few weeks insce, Mrs. Tur-ner, wife of Joseph Turner, Esq. (eulogy)

Issue of September 24, 1816

Married in Columbia, on Thursday evening last, Mr. David Ewa Merchant, to Miss Nancy Beeket.

Died on the 10th inst., in the 38th year of his age, Gen. Joseph Alston, late governor of this State. (long eulogy)

Issue of October 1, 1816

Married in Columbia, on Thursday evening last, Mr. David Beeket, to Miss Mary Rabb.

Issue of October 8, 1816

Married on Wednesday evening last, by the Rev. Dr. Maxcy, Mr. Michael J. Rudulph, printer, to Miss Louisa Maria Hendrick, both of this place.

Died on the 9th ult., at Albany, Gen. K. Van Rensselaeh. The general went early into the army during the War of Independence ...received a wound... The ball was never extracted until since his death, when it was taken out by Dr. Wm. Bay....

Issue of October 15, 1816

Married in Barnwell village, on Wednesday evening, the 25th of September, by the Rev. Daniel Brown, Mr. Barnet H. Brown, to the amiable Miss Louisa C. Duncan, both of that place.

On the same evening, by the Rev. Joshua Sharp, Mr. John H. Murphy of Beaufort District, to Miss Eliza Cannon of Barnwell District.

Died at sea, on the 22d July last, Burridge Purvis, Esq., in the 26th year of his age...a native of Scotland, and several years a respectable inhabitant of this place...left a widow and 8 children. (eulogy)

Issue of November 5, 1816

Married in Columbia, on Thursday night last, by the Rev. Mr. John Capers, the Rev. William Capers of Sumter District to Miss Susan M'Gill of this place.

Death of George Madison, governor of this state. He died on Monday last at Paris, Bourbon County; the government will be administered by Gabriel Slaughter, lt. gov. Ken. pa.

Issue of November 19, 1816

Died in Pendleton District, on the 29th ult., after an afflicting illness of 30 days, Mrs. Frances W. Tillinghast, wife of Daniel H. Tillinghast, Esq.

On the 6th November, at his seat at Morrissania, West Chester, the Hon. Governeur Morris, in the 65th year of his age.

Issue of August 17, 1819

Died at Columbia on Saturday evening last, after a very short illness, Miss Caroline A. Frazer, daughter of the late Dr. James Frazer.

Died on Saturday last, Master Isaac M'Pherson, a Student in College, son of Gen. Isaac M'Pherson.

Issue of June 12, 1821

Married on Thursday the 13th inst., by John Cherry, Esq., Mr. Daniel Brenan, a native of Ireland, to Miss Mary Edwards, youngest daughter of the late John Edwards, dec. all residents of Chester district.

TELESCOPE

Issue of June 12, 1821 (contd.)

Died, suddenly, on Sunday evening last, at the Saluda Public Works, near Columbia, Mr. Patrick M'Namara, a native of Ireland. At Beaufort, on the 17th instant, after an illness of only thirty-four hours, Michael O'Donovan, Esq.,Principal of Beaufort College, and for many years a respectable inhabitant of that place and Charleston.

Issue of October 1, 1822

Died on the 16th inst., at Mr. Stephen Garrett's, Edgefield District,S. C., Doctor William Howell Hay.
In Alabama, on Sunday evening, the 8th ult., Mrs. Mary W. Yancey, consort of John Yancey, esq., late Sheriff of Monroe Count in that state.
At his residence in Camden, S. C., Mr. John Nixon, son of Col. Wm. Nixon of that town. (eulogy)

Issue of May 29, 1824

Married by Wm. T. Woodward, Esq., on the 21st inst.,Mr. John Dunlapp to Miss Mary Hendrix, all of Fairfield District.

Issue of November 24, 1824

Married in Newberry district, on Sunday evening, the 13th inst., by the Rev. Nathan Boyd, Mr. Joel Graham, to Miss Nancy Reid.
Died on the 4th inst.,in Abbeville district, after a long and painful illness, Col. John Weatherall, in the 63d year of his age. In early life, he was one of those brave men who bore the burthen and heat of the day in the arduous struggle for in-dependence....

Issue of September 9, 1825

Died on the 19th ult., at his residence in Pendleton District Major Michael Dickson, in the 95th year of his age...a native of Ireland, came to America with his father and the age of 5 years, to the State of Pennsylvania....In 1777, he accepted a captaincy in the service of Georgia... Pendleton Messenger

Issue of January 13, 1826

Died at his residence in Fairfield, on the 3rd inst., Major James Goodwyn, in the 58th year of his age.
On the 3rd inst., at Darlington Courhouse, S. C., Henrietta Ellen, infant daughter of Dr. Thomas J. Flinn, of that place.

Issue of January 31, 1826

Died on the 13th of Jan., at her residence in Columbia, Miss Georgianna Virginia Blackburn, daughter of the late Professor Blackburn.

TELESCOPE

Issue of February 7, 1826

Died in Charleston, on the 16th instant, after a lingering illness...Theodore Gourdin, Sen., in the 62nd year of his age. (eulogy).

Issue of February 14, 1826

Died at his residence in the village of Edgefield, on the 2d inst., Edmund Bacon, sen., in the 51st year of his age...At an early age Mr. Bacon commenced the practice of Law in Savannah, Georgia; removed to Carolina about the year 1809....head and father of a respectable family.

Issue of February 28, 1826

Married in Fairfield, on the 16th inst, Mr. James Kilgore, to Miss Eliza M'Cullough, daughter of James M'Cullough, Esq., all of Fairfield.

Married at Greenville C. H., on the 21st inst.,by the Rev. Wm. B. Johns, Tandy Walker, Esq.,to Miss Mary H. Toney, both of this Village.

Issue of March 7, 1826

Died at his residence near Lancasterville, S. C., on the 20th Feb. last, Robert M. Crockett, Esq., formerly a member of the State Legislature.

Issue of March 14, 1826

Married in Union District, on Thursday the 23rd ult., by the Rev. Thomas Green, John Bates, Esq., to Miss Mary, daughter of Mr. Isaac Pearson, both of the same district.

Died in this place on Wednesday, the 8th instant, Mrs. Catharine Briggs, consort of Wm. Briggs. She was a native of Philadelphia and died in the 33d year of her age, after a residence of two years in this place...left an aged parent, six children and a bereaved husband....

Issue of March 28, 1826

Died at his residence in Fairfield District, 22 miles from Camden, of a severe and painfull illness which he bore with christian fortitude, Major William A. A. Belton, aged 23 years. He left a wife and one child....

Issue of April 4, 1826

Married on Thursday evening last, by the Rev. Mr. Folker, Mr. David Ewart to Mrs. Sophia Laval--all of this place.

Died in this place, on the 12th ult.,Mr. William Adger, of Fairfield, the eldest son of William Adger, Esq., of said district, aged 27 years... An affectionate wife and three small children live to attest his ardent and parental zeal for their future welfare...

35

Issue of April 11, 1826

Died on the 12th inst. near Statesburg at "Marden," the residence of his father, Wilson Waties, Esq., aged 23 years...He had just commenced the profession of the law.

Departed this transitory life on the 20th inst. at his residence in Newberry District, Mr. Walter Goodman, in the 76th year of his age...a native of Ireland, but for the last forty-five yea: a citizen of the United States.

Issue of April 18, 1826

Died at Camden, S. C., on the 6th instant, of the prevailing influenza, William Ennis, Printer, a native of Newbern, N. C., ag 32 years.

Issue of April 25, 1826

Died at Winnsborough, on the 29th ult., at the age of about 26, Mr. George Fitz, a graduate of Iartmouth College, New Hampshire, and late principal of Mout Sion College in Winnsborough.

Died on the 11th inst., at his residence in Greenville Distri Capt. Samuel Townes, aged fifty-three. As a husband, father, and friend, there wer but few equal, superior none.

Issue of May 2, 1826

Died at Edgefield C. H. on the 22d instant, Mrs. Elizabeth Tutt, consort of the late Richard Tutt, Esq., former Clerk of the Court at that place... She ahred with her husband, who bore a commission, in the cause of our common country, the many privatio incident to the campaigns of our revolutionary struggle, and was emphatically an American Heroine. She had entered upon her 68th year.

Died on the 1st ult., at her residence in this district, Mrs. W. Parrot, in the 65th year of her age. She was an affectionate wife and tender mother....

Issue of May 9, 1826

Died on Friday, the 21st of April, at her residence in Lauren District, S. C., Mrs. Elizabeth G. Ceason, wife of Josiah Ceason, Esq., in the 26th year of her age...left four children. Her parents, husband, and children are left to mourn...

Issue of May 23, 1826

Married on the third inst., by the Rev. Mr. Morgan, Samuel B. Wilkins, Esq., to Miss Mary Lee, all of Darlington District.

Died in Fayetteville, N. C.,on the 17th ult., Mr. Wm. M. Dunn son of the Rev. Jno M. Dunn.

Departed this life, on the 6th instant, at the residence of h husband, Colonel Frank Butler, in Edgefield District, Mrs.Louisa Butler, in the 29th year of her age...left a husband and four interesting children (the youngest about three days old at her death).

TELESCOPE

Issue of June 6, 1826

Died in this place, on the 4th instant, after a lingering illness of ten days, Mr. George C.Van Lew, aged 29 years. The deceased was a native of this state, but recently from Alabama....

Issue of June 13, 1826

Just as we were closing the columns of this days paper, the
death of Neil M'Farland was announced. Mr. F. was a native of
North Carolina, but for a long time past a resident of this place.

Issue of June 20, 1826

Departed this life on Monday the 12th instant, in this town,
in the twenty-seventh year of his age, Mr. Neil L. M'Farland, of
the frim of Latta & M'Farland, merchants. He was a native of
Richmond County, North Carolina, but had resided in this place
for eight years.... He was a worthy and beloved member of the
Presbyterian Church, of the Masonic Lodge, and of the Republican
Light Infantry of Columbia...left a young and affectionate wife....

Issue of June 27, 1826

Married on Sunday evening last, in the Episcopal Church, by
the Rev. Mr. Folker, Rev. William S. Wilson to Miss Eliza Blackburn, all of this place.

Issue of July 11, 1826

Married in Union District, on Tuesday evening, the 20th ult.,
by the Rev. Thos. Greer, Mr. James M. Whitlow to Miss Sarah Bobo,
all of that district.
Married on Thursday the 29th ult., by the Rev. Wm. West, Mr.
Sidney M. Davis to Miss Ann Salley, both of Orangeburgh district.

Issue of July 18, 1826

Married on Sunday the 2d instant, by the Rev. Mr. Holmes, Mr.
John Bow, to Miss Elizabeth Evans, all of this place.
Died on the 7th instant, Andrew Billings, a native of New
London County, Connecticut, but for several years a resident of
this place--he sustained the character of an honest man.

Issue of August 8, 1826

Married on the 18th ult., by the Rev.R. B. Walker, J. D. Witherspoon, Esq., to Miss Ann T. K. Reid, all of York District.
Died in this place on Saturday last, 5th inst., Mr. John Pagand,
supposed to be about 34 years of age. Mr. P. is a native of Norfolk in Virginia, but for some time past has been a resident of
this town.
Another Revolutionary Hero Gone. Died at his residence at
Sligo, on Monday evening, the 34d July, Col. Henry Hampton, in
the 74th year of his age. Col. Hampton was one of the few surviving officers of the revolutionary army.... At the battles of the
Eutaw Springs and Camden, his conduct has long been known as that
of a brave and distinguisehd officer. Woodville (Miss.) Rep.

TELESCOPE

Issue of August 29, 1826

Departed this life on Friday last, after an illness of 3 days
Mr. John Robson, an enterprising merchant of this place, in his
33d year... Mr. Robson was born in England, but the home of his
birth was not the place for his free and enterprising spirit.
For the past 8 years he has been a resident amongst us...leaving
behind an affectionatebrother...buried in the Episcopal Churchyar

Issue of September 5, 1826

Married on Tuesday evening last, by the Rev. Mr. Clifton, Mr.
William Myers, to Miss Eliza, daughter of Major John M'Lemore of
this District.

Issue of September 19, 1826

These reflections have been suggested by the death of the
two interesting children of Mr. William Hilliary of this place,
who both died suddenly on Tuesday and Wednesday the 12th and 13th
instant. Thomas, aged about six years...died Tuesday about noon.
Martha, aged about three years...about noon on Wednesday.
Died in this place on the 14th inst., Mrs. Hollan Bowie, wife
of Mr. Benjamin Bowie.
Departed this life on Friday the 1st inst., in the prime of
life, Samuel M'Creary Jr., Post Master at Beckhamville, aged 35
years and three months. He has left a disconsolate wife and two
small children....

Issue of September 26, 1826

Died on the 22nd inst., after an illness of near a month, Mr.
Stephen W. Doan, a native of Tenn., but for many years an inhabi-
tant of this place, in the 25th year of his age.
In this place on Sunday night last, Mr. James Stark, son of
Robert Stark, Esq., in the 19th year of his age.
Near this place, on Tuesday last, Mr. Dan'l Acy, in his
twenty-fourth year, Mr. A. was a native of England and maintained
the character of an honest man.

Issue of October 3, 1826

Died in the 26th year of his age, Thomas G. Reynolds, a nativ
of Wallingford, Conn., but for a number of years an inhabitant of
this place. Mr. Reynolds has left a disconsolate widow and two
infant children, with a number of relatives....
Died at his residence in Laurens district, on the 21st ult.,
Capt. Thomas Ligon.

Issue of October 10, 1826

Died on Monday the 2d inst., Miss Harriet Hampton, eldest
daughter of Gen. Wade Hampton of this place.
On Thursday morning last, at his summer residence in Fairfiel
district, Maj. Claiborn Clifton.
At Lebanon Springs, N. Y., on the 22d ult., Hon. William Craf
of Charleston.

TELESCOPE

Issue of October 17, 1826

Died in Philadelphia, on the 3rd inst., Mr. William Purvis, for many years a respectable inhabitnat of our town, in the 64th year of his age.

Issue of October 24, 1826

Died on the 16th inst., at his summer residence in Lexington district, Col. Jacob Countz, aged 34 years.

Issue of November 7, 1826

Died in Fairfield district, on the 23rd ult., Mrs. Nancy Picket, wife of Mr. Jephthah Picket, and daughter of Mr. Musco, in the 39th year of her age. Mrs. P. has left seven children, five daughters and two sons....

Issue of November 14, 1826

Departed this life on the 6th instant, Mrs. Elizabeth F. Holmes, wife of James G. Holmes, Esq., and daughter of Judge DeSaussure, in the 29th year of her age....
Tribute of Respect to Alfred Hampton by the Columbia Male Academy.

Issue of November 21, 1826

Died on Thursday the 9th inst., at his father's residence, Stephen W. Carwile, eldest son of John S.Carwile, Esq., late sheriff of Newberry district. He had just entered his fifteenth year.
Died at her residence in Abbeville district, on the 8th instant, Delphia Adelia, the wife of Capt. A. C. Hamilton, aged 39 years... left a husband and large family of children....

Issue of January 18, 1827

Married on Tuesday, 7th inst., by the Rev. W. Belshre, Mr. Joseph L. Bowhillon to Miss M. F. Gardnier, all of Abbeville District, 4½ miles below Willington, S. C.

Issue of February 1, 1827

Died at her residence in Abbeville District, after a very short illness, on the 20th ult., Mrs. Susan W. Logan, wife of Dr. John Logan, in the 28th year of her age. She has left a doating husband and two lovely children...member of the Methodist Church.

Issue of February 8, 1827

Married in Union District on Thursday evening, the 23rd inst., by the Rev. Mr. Ray, Capt. Robert M'Collough of Newberry, to Miss Elizabeth Wallace of Union District.
Married on the 1st inst., by the Right Rev. Bishop Bowen, Edward Rutledge Laurens, Esq., to Miss Margaret Horry Horry, daughter of Elias L. Horry, Esq., all of Charleston.
Died on his way from Union to Columbia, after a short illness, in the house of Mr. Veal, Wm. F. Gist, a citizen of Union District.

Issue of February 15, 1827

Married on Thursday evening last, the 8th inst., by the Rev.
Dr. Gadsden, Dr. James Ramsay, to Eleanor, daughter of the late
Henry Laurens, Esq.,all of Charleston.

Issue of March 8, 1827

Died in this place on the evening of the 6th inst., in the
23rd year of his age, Mr. James Mollan, a native of New York.
Died in this place on the morning of the 2nd inst., Mr.
William Miller, a gallant Soldier of the Revolution....

Issue of March 22, 1827

Married on Thursday evening,the 15th inst., by the Rev. W.
Paulling, Mr. Samuel P. Corbin to Miss Caroline M. Saylor, both
of Lexington District.
Died at her residence in Lexington District on the 22d February
Mrs. Lavina Taylor, relict of Wm. Taylor. Mrs. T. was well stricke
in years.

Issue of May 3, 1827

Departed this life on the morning of the 13th inst., at his
residence in Union District, Mr. William C. Glenn, in the 67th
year of his age. Mr. Glenn was a native of Virginia, and emigrated
to S. C. shortly after the close of the revolutionary war...left
widow and eight children.
Married on Thursday evening last, by the Rev. Mr. Mallory, Mr.
Joseph Brevard to Miss Keziah Hopkins.
On Thursday evening last, by the Rev. Mr. Folker, Mr. Willis
White to Miss Louisa Sheppard.
On Thursday evening last, by the Rev. Mr. Tradewell, Mr. Reuber
House to Miss Eliza Dinkins.
On Tuesday morning, the 20th ult.,by the Rev. Mr. Folker, Mr.
James Daniel of Spartanburg to Mrs. Murdock of this place.
at Augusta, Ga., on Thursday the 19th ult., by the Rev. Mr.
Talmadge, Mr. Paul Fitzsimons to Miss Eleanor N. White.

Issue of May 11, 1827

Married last evening, by Professor Henry, Col. F. H. Elmore of
Walterborough, to Miss Harriet C. Taylor of this place.

Issue of May 18, 1827

Married on the evening of the 3rd inst., by the Rev. Mr.
Foulker, James Jones, Esq., of Edgefield to Miss Catherine Creyon
of this place.
On Tuesday evening last, by the Rev. Mr. Tradewell, Dr. James
C. Kennerly to Miss Catherine B. Smith.
Died on the 16th of April last, Mrs. Juliana Hoffman, relict
of Jacob Hoffman, of Orangeburgh District, aged 37 years and 5
months...
Drowned on Saturday last, while bathing in the river near this
place, Mr. John Lofton...member of the Senior Class of South-Carolina College.

Issue of June 1, 1827

Married on Thursday the 17th ult., by the Rev. Mr. Paulding, Mr. John Scott to Miss Ann Carter, all of this district.

On Thursday the 24th ult., by the Rev. Mr. Tradewell, Mr. Charles Howell to Mrs. ___ Kester, all of this district.

Issue of June 8, 1827

Married in Union district, on Tuesday the 29th ult.,by the Rev. Mr. Russel, Clough S. Meng, Esq., to Miss Mary Giles.

Died at Providence, R. I., Lt. Pardon M. Whipple of the U. S. Navy, in the 37th year of his age....

Issue of June 15, 1827

Died at Smithfield, N. C., on the 19th ult., Mr. Richard Gutsell, aged about 26, a native of Sussex County, England.

Issue of June 22, 1827

Married on Thursday, the 7th inst.,by the Rev. Mr. Mallary, Mr. William Flowers to Miss Martha Hollinshead, all of this district.

Issue of June 29, 1827

Died in this place, on Sunday last, Mrs. Mourning Mullion, in the 36th year of her age.

Issue of July 6, 1827

Married in this place on Thursday evening last, by the Rev. Mr. Folker, Mr. William Briggs, formerly of Philadelphia, to Mrs. Lydia M. Brown, of Rahway, N. Jersey.

Died in this town on the 24th of June, Mrs. Jane Marks, wife of Dr. Elias Marks, aged 39...a native of Boston, in Lincolnshire, England....

Issue of July 13, 1827

Died on Saturday, the 5th inst., at the residence of Mr. John Glover, Mary, daughter of James and Elizabeth Mobley, aged 13 months.

Issue of July 27, 1827

Married on Monday evening last, by the Rev. P. H. Folker, Dr. Edward Sill to Miss Caroline M. Greenwood, all of this place.

In Fairfield district, S. C., on Thursday evening, the 19th inst., by the Rev. Samuel W. Yongue, Mr. Daniel Hall, to Miss Mary, second daughter of Thomas M'Collough, merchant of Fairfield district.

Died in this place, on the 20th inst., Napoleon B., infant son of D. E. & C. Sweeny, aged 2 years, 10 months and six days.

In Newberry district, S. C., Dr. Reuben Flanagan, of whom it emphatically may be said, he lived respected and died lamented....

Issue of August 10, 1827

Died in Lancaster District, on the 17th ult., after a long

and severe illness, Mr. Matthew Sims, in the 51st year of his age...left a large family to lament his loss.
Died in Augusta, Ga., on the 2d inst., Mr. Doyle S. Goolrick, aged twenty six years, a native of Fredericksburg, Va.

Issue of August 24, 1827

Died at his summer residence, near Totness, in St. Matthew's Parish, on Friday last, John Louisa Raoul, de Champmanoir, in the 44th year of his age. Born of an ancient and illustrious family in France....In 1813, he married in this State, a lady of wealth and respectability, who with six children now deplore his death.
Died on the 15th inst., Mrs. Mary Ann Harris, wife of Dr. B. F. Harris.
Died in Charleston, on the 16th inst., Mr. John W. Black, son of Mr. John Black, merchant, of this place, in the 19th year of his age...visited Charleston for the purpose of completing his medical studies....

Issue of August 31, 1827

Died on Monday the 20th inst., Mrs. Martha Fullerton Rogers, wife of John Rogers of Fairfield District, in the 30th year of her age. She was a native of the State of Pennsylvania, and for twelve years past a citizen of South Carolina....

Issue of September 21, 1827

Departed this life on Saturday the 10th inst., Miss Nancy Parrot, daughter of Mr. Thos. Parrot of this district....
Died in Edgefield District, on Tuesday the 11th inst., Miss Elizabeth J. Bonham, aged 18 years.
Died in Yorkville, on Saturday morning, the 8th inst., Mrs. Maryy Ann D., consort of Andrew mcWhorter, Esq., of that village, aged 27 years....

Issue of September 28, 1827

Died in this place, on the 22nd inst., Mr. William McCauley, merchant, aged 32 years. This melancholy event was the consequen of an injury recieved about thirty hours previous to his dissolu- tion....

Issue of October 5,1827

Married on Thursday the 20th ult., by the Rev. Mr. Folker, Alexander Herbemont, Esq., to Miss Martha Davis Bay, all of Columbia.

Issue of October 19, 1827

Married on Thursday evening last, by the Rev. Mr. Folker, Mr. Peter Clissey to Miss Jane Seybt, all of this place.
On Wednesday evening, the 17th inst., by the Rev. Mr. Folker, Col. Esek H. Maxcy, to Miss Elizabeth Dinkins, all of this place.
On Thursday evening, the 18th inst., by the Rev. Mr. Tradewel Mr. John J. Rawls of Columbia, to Miss Ann Elizabeth Geiger, of Lexington.
In this district on the 9th inst., by the Rev. Mr. Mallory, James L. Clark, Esq., to Mrs. Martha S. Scott, all of this distri
on the 10th ult., in Chester District, by the Rev. W. S. Wils

Walter Izard, Esq., to Miss Mary Cadwallader, daughter of Allen Jones Green.

Issue of October 26, 1827

Died in Charleston on the 16th inst., Miss Joannah England, sister of Bishop England.

Issue of November 2, 1827

Married in Orangeburgh District on the 25th of October, by the Rev. Mr. Murrowe, Mr. Joseph Pou, to Miss Eliza M. Felder.

Died at her residence in Laurens District, S. C., on the 22nd ult., Elenor Garlington, widow of Edwin Garlington, in the 56th year of her age.

Died on Horn's Creek, in Edgefield District, S. C., on the 3rd ult., Capt. John Ryan, a distinguished patriot of the Revolution, in the 85th year of his age. (long account).

Issue of November 9, 1827

Married in Spartanburg district, on the 16th ult., by the Rev. Mr. ----, Mr. Thomas F. Murphy to Miss Elizabeth W. Farrow.

Died in this place, on the 1st inst., of Pulmonary consumption, at the residence of Doctor Wells, John W. Robeson, M. D., in the 23rd year of his age.

Issue of November 16, 1827

Died at the house of Mr. Jesse Goodwyn, Mrs. Mary T. Hopkins, in the 58th year of her age.

Issue of November 22, 1827

Married on Thursday evening last, by the Rev. Mr. Hanckell, Charles R. Carroll, Esq., to Sarah F., daughter of the late Major Francis B. Fishburn.

On Thursday evening last, by the Rev. Dr. Dalcho, George B. Ried, Esq., to Miss Eliza Smith, third daughter of Dr. John Ramsay--all of Charleston.

Issue of December 10, 1827

Died in this town on Monday morning, 3d inst., Mrs. Eliza Hilleary, aged 28 years, consort of Mr. William Hilleary, formerly of New York.

Issue of December 13, 1827

Died in this District on the 7th inst., Wm. Devlin, Esq., born in Abbeville District in this state.

Issue of December 21, 1827

Died on Tuesday afternoon, last after a long and severe illness, Gen. J. J. Faust, of this town....

Issue of December 28, 1827

Died on Sunday, Dec. 23rd, 1827, of Typhys fever, Mr. James C. Keith, student of the South Carolina College.

Issue of January 2, 1829

Married on the 24th ult., at Orangeburgh, by the Rev. John Murrowe, Sermon Bonsall (formerly of Philadelphia) to Miss C. P. Jennings.

On the 22d of December, by the Rev. Mr. CAmpbell, John F. G. Mittag, Attorney at Law, to Miss Ann M'Kenna, only daughter of Mr. Wm. M'Kenna, all of Lancasterville, S. C.

Died on the 8th December last, at her residence in Saluda river, in Edgefield district, Mrs. Nancy Mays, late consort of General Samuel Mays, deceased....arrived at a considerable old age, and was the mother of a numerous family...member of the Baptist Church.

Issue of February 20, 1829

Died at his residence in Granby on Friday evening, the 13th inst., of a lingering illness, Mr. Nicholas Hane, at the venerable age of 81....

Issue of March 6, 1829

Married In New York on Wednesday, the 4th ult., by the Rev. Mr. Hart, Mr. Joshua P. Norane, to Miss Catharine, eldest daughter of Henry Lazarus of this place.

Issue of March 13, 1829

Married on Tuesday evening, February 24th, in Newberry Village by the Rev. Mr. Saml. P. Pressly, Dr. James H. Wilson, to Miss Elizabeth F. Harrington, eldest daughter of Y. J. Harrington, Esq.

by the same, on Thursday the 26th of February at the residence of Dr. C. B. Atwood, in Newberry District, Dr. Thomas B. Rutherford, to Miss Laura Adams, eldest daughter of Dr. Adams, deceased, late of Newberry Village.

Died at his residence in Lexington District, on the 3d inst., at an advanced age, Mr. Wm. Baker, Sen., one of the oldest and most respectable inhabitants of that district.

Issue of March 20, 1829

Died on Sunday the 8th inst., Alexander Crumpton, Esq., at his residence in Fairfield dist., in his 59th year...a zealous, orderly, and consistent member of the Baptist Church for more than 23 years...office of a Deacon....

Issue of March 27, 1829

Died on the 19th inst., at his residence in Edgefield District Col. Mathias Jones in the 53d year of his age.

Issue of April 3, 1829

Died on the 30th ult., after a short illness, Mrs. Maria Preston, wife of Col. Wm. C. Preston, in the 37th year of her age.

Died, by accidnet, at his residence in Alabama, George C. Player, formerly a citizen of this state.

TELESCOPE

Issue of April 10, 1829

Departed this life on the 21st of March, Major John Nesbit, of Lancaster District, S. C. Major Nesbit was one among the first in this section of the country, to support the cause of independence in our revolutionary struggle. He fought in most of the engagements in the upper part of the state...elected to the Legislature of this State, and many other district appointements. He died in his 70th year....

Died on the 25th ult., Mrs. Elizabeth, consort of Hugh Milling, of Fairfield district, at quite an advanced age....

Issue of May 8, 1829

Died on the 15th inst., at his residence in Lexington District, Mr. George Eigleberger, in the 47th year of his age...a humane and forbearing master to his slaves....

Issue of May 22, 1829

Married in Fairfield dist. on Tuesday the 14th inst., by the Rev. Mr. Means, Mr. Thomas Lauderdale, to Miss Mary McMillan.

In Winnsborough, on Thursday the 14th inst., by the Rev. Mr. Braieley, Mr. John Woodward, to Miss Mary Rebecca Pearson.

Near Monticello, Fairfield District, on Tuesday the 19th inst., by the Rev. Mr. Holmes, Doct. Joel E. Pearson to Miss Ann Weston.

Issue of June 5, 1829

Married on the 27th ult., by the Rev. Mr. Converse, the Hon. George McDuffie to Miss Mary Rebecca Singleton, daughter of Richard Singleton, Esq. of Sumter District.

Issue of June 19, 1829

Died on the 6th instant, in his 60th year, Mr. Isaac Frazier, an old inhabitant of Columbia.

Departed this life in Lancaster dist., on the 4th inst., Mrs. Comfort Ann Barber, consort of Nath'l Barber, aged 49 years and 8 months..

Issue of July 3, 1829

Died on the 14th ult., in the 36th year of her age, Mrs. Eliza Sanders Guignard, consort of James S. Guignard, Esqr., of this town.

Married on the 16th inst., in Fairfield dist., Mr. J. E. Peay, to Miss Elizabeth Ellison, daughter of Mr. William Ellison.

Issue of July 10, 1829

Died on the evening of the 25th of June, in Union dist., Mrs. Elizabeth D. Benson, wife of Abner Benson, Esq., and eldest daughter of Gen. Elijah Dawkins. Mrs. Benson had recently given birth to two infant children....

Issue of July 24, 1829

Married on Thursday, the 11th ult., by the Rev. Jesse Heart-well, Elias D. Earle, Esq., of Greenville, S. C., to Miss Susan C. Haynsworth, eldest daughter of Dr. James Haynsworth, of Sumter ville.

Departed this life on Friday the 9th inst., Mr. Elisha Hammon superintendant of the Macon academy, in the 53rd year of his age Mr. Hammond was born in Massachusetts, in the year 1776, and aft receiving a collegiate education at Dartmouth College, he emigra to South Carolina, when he was called to take charge of Mount Bethel Academy...professor of languages in South Carolina Colleg From Carolina he removed to Georgia, and after a short time spen in Augusta, accepted an invitation to take charge of the Macon Academy, and in June 1828 became a citizen of this place...left a widow and four children. Macon paper.

Issue of August 21, 1829

Died at St. Augustine, East Florida, on the 26th July last, L. H. Coe, formerly of this town, in the 46th year of his age.

Issue of August 28, 1829

Died in Columbia, on the evening of the 25th inst., after an illness of nine days, Thomas F. Taylor, the second son of Maj. Thomas Taylor, jun. of this place, and a member of the Junior Class of the South Caroline College. He was in his 20th year...

Died at Rice's in Laurens district, on the 14th inst., Miss Lucy B. Herndon, youngest daughter of Col. Berry Herndon, dec'd Newberry district....

Died in Columbia, on the 27th instant, Mr. John G. Walsh, fo merly of this place, and lately a citizen of Augusta.

Issue of September 4, 1829

Died at his residence near this place on Monday, the 3rd ins of Bilious Cholic, Mr. Richard H. Harrison, in the 44th year of his age. The deceased was a native of South Carolina, and emigrated to Alabama among the first settlers of the county of Tuskaloosa, where he resided for some years, and thence removed to the place which knew him last.... Alabama Spectator.

Issue of September 11, 1829

Died at Plane Hill, near Camden, on the 2nd day of September the infant son of Gov. Miller, aged four weeks.

On Saturday, the 9th inst., of Consumption, at the house of Mr. Davis near this place, Mrs. Mary Catharine Ann Moore, in the 20th year of her age, wife of Mr. John D. Moore of Charleston, and only daughter of Mr. M. M'Elroy of this place.

Issue of September 25, 1829

Married on Tuesday the 8th inst., by the Rev. Mr. Boyd, Mr. Arch. Hannah to Miss Susannah, eldest daughter of Wm. Herrons, Esq., all of Fairfield District.

On Thursday evening, the 17th inst., by the Rev. Mr. Boyd, Mr. Robert Bell to Miss Nancy M'Dowell, all of Fairfield Distric

Issue of October 9, 1829

Died at his residence in Lexington District, on the evening of the 6th inst., Col. John W. Lee, in the 45th year of his age, leaving a widow and a numerous family....

On Thursday the 24th ult., at her residence in Sumter District, in the 21st year of her age, Mrs. Eliza L. Spann, wife of Richard R. Spann, and only daughter of Robert Weston, Jun., of Richland District....

Issue of October 16, 1829

Died at his residence in Newberry District, Mr. Thomas Oadel, in the 38th year of his age.

At the same place, on the same day, Miss Sarah, daughter to Capt. Jacob and Sarah Duckett, in the 19th year of her age.

In Union District, on the 20th inst., at his residence the Cross-Keys, Capt. Barram Bobo, in the 54th year of his age.

In York District, on Sunday the 11th instant, Mrs. Mary Bailey, wife of Thomas Bailey Sen. She was an aged lady.

Died in this place, on Sunday last, Mr. John Bow.

Issue of October 23, 1829

Departed this life on the 15th inst., at the residence of her husband, Mr. George Free, in Fairfield District, Mrs. Nancy Free, in the 57th year of her age.

Issue of November 6, 1829

Married in Newberry village, on the 27th October, by the Rev. Samuel P. Pressly, Spencer C. Harrington, Esq., to Miss Mary B. Maxwell, all of Newberry village.

Issue of November 13, 1829

Died at his residence in Lexington Dist., near Savannah Hunt, Mr. Henry Geiger, in the 75th year of his age. His numerous children and relatives will long revere his memory....

The Port Gibson Correspondent and other Mississippi papers will confer a peculiar act of kindness by copying the above notice in thier papers, to the end that it may meet the attention of a descendant of the deceased, supposed to be resident in that state.

Issue of November 20, 1829

Died in Abbeville district, on Thursday, the 4th instant, the Rev. James Crowther, in the 65th year of his age. The deceased emigrated from England during the Revolutionary war and settled in Abbeville. He belonged to the Baptist Church of which he had been a member upwards of 35 years....

Issue of December 1, 1829

Died in Newberry District, on the 15th instant, Mrs. Mary Glenn, in the 51st year of her age....

Issue of December 20, 1831

Married in Wiansborough, on Wednesday evening, the 14th inst by the Rev. Mr. Brairly, Dr. Caleb Clarke to Miss Cynthia Woodwa
On Tuesday evening, the 13th inst., by the Revd. Mr. Boyd, M Thomas Barkley to Miss Carolina Martin, all of Fairfield Distric

Issue of October 9, 1832

Married on Tuesday evening, the 25th ult., by John Knox, Esq Mr. Daniel Quattlebaum of Lexington District to Miss Sophia Love lace of Edgefield.

Issue of November 27, 1832

Married on Thursday, 1st inst., by the Rev. Mr. Hope, John R. Dreher to Miss Rebecca, eldest daughter of Col. West Caughman all of Lexington District.
On the same day, by Rev. Thomas Rall, John Fox, Esq., to Mis Eliza, daughter of Thomas K. Poindexter, of Lexington District.
On Thursday, 8th inst., by Rev. Mr. Adams, Mr. Jacob Harman, to Miss Mahala Edwards, all of Lexington village.
Died at his father's residence in Fairfield District, on the night of the 18th inst., Mr. Andrew Bradford, in the 20th year o his age....

Issue of January 29, 1833

Married on the 21st inst., by the Rev. Mr. Freeman, Mr. Robe T. Preston of Virginia, to Miss Mary Hart, daughter of Major B. Hart of Lexington.
On the 24th inst., by the Rev. Mr. Means, Mr. John Means to Miss Sarah Stark.
On the 24th inst.,by the Rev. G. Duke, the Rev. J. C. Hope to Miss Louisa Egleburger, all of Lexington district.

Issue of March 12, 1833

Died in this place on the 22nd ult., John R. Davis, Esq., la a member of the Columbia bar....
At Milwood, the seat of her husband, Col. Wade Hampton, near this place, on the 27th of February last, Mrs. Ann Hampton, in the 39th year of her age.... This event has deprived of a mother care nine children, the youngest of whom is but an infant, and the eldest not beyond the age of maternal control....

Issue of March 26, 1833

Married in Fayette County, West Florida, on the 18th inst., Col. Isaac Fort of Jackson county to Miss Jane Caroline, daughter of Col. Wm. Toney, of the former county.
In Fayette County, West Florida, on the same evening, Mr. Robert G. Ricks, of Jackson County, to Miss Eliza Emily, daughter of Col. William Toney of the former county.
In Columbia on the 14th inst., by the Rev. J. C. Kennedy, Mr. John Donaldson to Miss Margaret Brown, all of this place.
On Wednesday the 20th in Fairfield district, by Thos Lumpkin, Esq., Mr. John Coates of Kershaw to Miss Martha Henson of Fairfie
On Thursday 21st inst., in Fairfield district, at the house c Mr. Wm. Lewis, by Wm. Hemphill, Esq., Mr. Wm. Wall of Chester

District to Miss Emelia Pickett of Fairfield.

On Friday the 22nd inst., in Fairfield, at the house of Mr.
Wm. Lewis, by John Gunthrop, Esq., Mr. John B. Pickett to Miss
Susanna Watson, all of Fairfield.

Issue of April 2, 1833

Died in Columbia, Mrs. Mary McDowell, wife of Alexander Mc-
Dowell. In early life she became a member of the Methodist Church.
She departed this life the 12th inst. after a severe and protrac-
ted illness....

Issue of April 9, 1833

Departed this life on Saturday, March 30th, at Granby, Mrs.
Narcissa Sondley, wife of Mr. Richard Sondley of Columbia....

Issue of April 16, 1833

Married on the 21st of March last, by the Rev. William C.
Bennet, Capt. Ephraim Faber to Miss Elizabeth Glimph, all of
Newberry District, South Carolina.

Issue of April 23, 1833

Died in Columbia, S. C., Richland district, at the residence
of her mother, on the 18th of April, and in the 22nd year of her
age, Mrs. Ann Brennan, wife of Mr. Thomas Brennan, formerly merchant in Columbia, but now residing in Montgomery, Alabama. Mrs.
Brennan was a lady of superior mind and strong intellectual powers.
After much reflection and acquaintance with the Catholic religion,
she made from conviction her profession of faith, and was received
into the Catholic church a few months previous to her death...left
a husband and child....

Issue of April 30, 1833

Married in Twiggs County, Georgia, on the 14th inst., Mr.
John Hamiter of the firm Friday & Hamiter, Columbia, S. C., to
Miss Prudence, daughter of Col. ---- Hodges of the former place.

Issue of May 7, 1833

Died at her residence in Newberry District, on the 22d April,
Mrs. Dorothy R. Wadlington, in the fifty first year of her age....

Issue of June 11, 1833

Died on the 25th May, at his plantation near Montgomery, Alabama, John MacIver, Esq.,a native of Scotland, and recently a
respectable Merchant of this place.

Issue of July 23, 1833

Married on Tuesday evening last, by the Rev. Thomas Ledbetter,
Mr. John C. Taylor to Miss Mary R. Livingston, all of this district.
On Saturday the 12th inst., by the Rev. Mr. English, Mr. Alexander McDowell, a resident of Columbia, to Miss Rebecca Kimble,
lately from Philadelphia.

Issue of July 30, 1833

Died on the 19th inst., in this place, Marie Martha Raynal, formerly of St. Domingo, about 100 years of age.

Issue of August 6, 1833

Married in the vicinity of Laurel Hill, Richmond county, on the 25th ult., by the Rev. Archibald McQueen, Mr. Benjamin L. McLauchlin, Merchant of Columbia, S. C., to Miss Eliza McLean, only daughter of Hugh McLean, Esq.

On Thursday evening, the 25th ult., by John Knox, Esq., Mr. John W. Cully to Miss Polly Quattlebom, all of Lexington district.

On Tuesday evening, the 30th ult., by the Rev. Bond English, Mr. Francis S. Bronson, Printer, to Miss Mary Tillery, both of this place.

Departed this life on Saturday 28th ult., Mr. James Watts Jr. eldest son of James Watts, Esq., of Laurens district, in the 38th year of his age...left a wife with six little children....

Issue of August 20, 1833

Married in Augusta, on Tuesday evening last, by the Rev. Mr. Barry, Mr. William H. Pritchard to Mrs. Jane Adelaide Dimon of the former place.

Issue of September 10, 1833

We greatly regret to state that the Hon. T. D. Singleton, who election to Congress it lately gave us so much pleasure to announ died last week, at Raleigh, while on his way to Washington City.

Issue of September 24, 1833

Departed this life at her residence in Fairfield District, on Thursday the 5th inst., after an illness of nearly five months, Mrs. Mary Harson, aged 73 years...a member of the Methodist Episcopal Church, for upwards of 10 years....

Issue of October 22, 1833

Married on Tuesday evening, the 15th inst., by the Rev. R. Means, Mr. Daniel H. Kew, to Mrs. Martha A. Wrench, both of Fairfield District.

Issue of November 5, 1833

Married on Wednesday the 30th by the Rev. Mr. English, Mr. James W. Pierce, to Miss Mary C. Faust, daughter of Mr. Daniel Faust, all of this place.

Issue of November 12, 1833

Married on the evening of the 29th ult., at Marden, near Stateburg, by the Rev. Mr. Converse, Doct. W. W. Anderson to Miss Elizabeth Waties, second daughter of the late Hon. Judge Waties.

In Jefferson Co. (Geo.) on the 26th ult., Mrs. Mary Ann Ramsay, aged 67, consort of the late Hon. Ephraim Ramsay of South Carolina.

Issue of November 12, 1833 (contd.)

Died in Clinton on the 3d inst., Mrs. Finch, consort of Mr. David Finch, formerly of this place.

Issue of November 19, 1833

Our Town has just followed to the grave, its Patriarch. The venerable Col. Thomas Taylor died, on Sunday morning, at the residence of his son, Mr. Benjamin Taylor, and was buried yesterday, in the family burying-ground.... Extended Biography in the issues of Nov. 25, 29 and Dec. 6.... born 10 Sept 1743, in Amelia County, Virginia. In 1754, his fahter emigrated to this state, on the eastern bank of the Congaree, 10 miles below Columbia. In 1766 married Miss Anne Wyche, of Brunswick (now Greenville) county, Va. (long account of Rev. service) Mrs. Taylor survives her husband, leaves 30 grandchildren and 20 great-grandchildren.

Issue of November 29, 1833

Died on the 21st inst., at his residence in Fairfield, Major Joshua Player, in the 57th year of his age.

Issue of December 6, 1833

Married in Lexington Dist.,on the 28th last month, by Esquire Fulmer, Mr. Nathan Lyles, to Miss T. Busby.

Died at his residence in Pickens district, on the 23d ult., Capt. Samuel Earle. At the age of 16, Capt. Earle enrolled himself in the service of his county, which he continued to the close of the Revolution. Capt. Earle was in active service during the whole war. At the close of the war, the late Gen. Butler and Capt. Earle were selected to command two companies of rangers for the protection of the interior from the ravages of Indians and Tories....

Died, very suddenly, in Fairfield, on the morning of the 7th last month, Mr. Stephen Gibson, Sen., in the 69th year of his age.

At Tomsville, in Chester District, on the 21st ult., William McCluney, in the 99th year of his age, a native of Ireland. He came to this state about the commencement of the Revolution, and when the British army invaded the state, he volunteered in her defence....

Issue of December 17, 1833

Robert M. Smith, second son of Mr. W. R. Smith, of Laurens District, died on Wednesday the 20th ultimo, aged 20 years. His nature was too sensitive for this world....

Issue of January 7, 1834

Died of consumption on the 1st instant, Miss Jane Arabella Faust, second daughter of Mr. Daniel Faust, of this town.

Issue of January 14, 1834

Died on Monday the 5th inst., at his residence in Fairfield District, Eugene Joseph Brevard, in the 30th year of his age (long eulogy).

In Columbia, Mrs. Sarah Adams, wife of Mr. John Adams, formerly of this place. By the death of this lady three small children have been left destitute; Mr. Adams having left this place, with the intention of returning, and nothing having been heard of him for some considerable time. It is hoped this notice may meet his eye, if living.

Issue of February 11, 1834

Married in Columbia, on the 4th inst., by the Rev. Benjamin Tradewell, Mr. Benjamin S. King, to Miss Sarah Ann Waddle.

Died on Saturday last, Mary Virginia, daughter of Mr. William Gregg of this place, aged 3 years and 6 months.

Issue of February 25, 1834

Married by the Rev. Mr. Hodges, on the 28th ult., Captain John D. Strother, of Fairfield, to Miss Harriet Pope of Newberry.

Died on the 20th inst., after a severe illness of a few days, Samuel Wilson, youngest son of Dr. Robert W. and C. E. Gibbes, aged 1 year and 14 days.

Issue of March 8, 1834

Married in this place on Thursday evening 27th February, by the Rev. Bond English, Mr. Jno. B. Steele of Barnwell to Miss Martha Maria Stanly, of Hayneville, Alabama, formerly of Columbia

On Thursday evening last, by the Rev. Benjamin Tradewell, Mr. E. F. Branthwaite, to Miss Caroline Harriet, daughter of Mr. John Parr.

Departed this life on the 8th ult., at her Father's, Col. Chappell's house in this place, Mrs. Eugenia Calhoun, wife of Andrew P. Calhoun, Esq. in the 22d year of her age. She was married only about 13 months...left a husband, and an infant daughter, parents and relatives....

Issue of June 7, 1834

Married near Ceader Shoals on Saturday, 24th ultimo, by Joseph McMullen, Esq., Mr. Alexander Crane to Miss Rebecca, only daughter of W. Heath, Esq., both of Chester District.

Issue of July 12, 1834

Married near M'Donald's Ferry, on the Catawba River, on Thursday, the 26th ult., by the Rev. Joseph T. Copeland, James M. Richardson, Esq. (Merchant of Lancasterville) to Miss Martha Matilda, daughter of Capt. John Gooch, of Chester District.

A tribute of respect to the memory of Dr. Thomas J. Broselman of Newberry District, a graduate of Lexington, Ky...died on the 25th April last in the 32nd year of his age....

Issue of July 19, 1834

Died on the 10th June, in Columbus, Geo., Mrs. Frances A. E.

Black, aged 22 years and a few months, daughter of Mr. John Mc-Morris, of Newberry, deceased, and wife of James Black, formerly of Columbia, South Carolina....

Died at Edgefield on the 16th instant, in the 23d year of her age, Mrs. Harriet Hayne Butler, wife of Judge Butler. (eulogy)

Issue of August 9, 1834

Married on Thursday the 7th inst., by the Rev. Mr. Tradewell, Mr. Jacob Bookman, of Fairfield district, to Miss Rebecca C. Chappell, of this district.

Died at his residence in Fairfield District on Wednesday the 30th of July, Samuel Alston, Esq., in the 65th year of his age... member of both branches of the Legislature.

Issue of August 30, 1834

Married on Thursday evening, 21st instant, by Thos. Williamson, Esq., Mr. Joseph Jordan, to Miss Elizabeth Ann Fouts, both of Orangeburg District.

Issue of September 6, 1834

Died at Dr. S. Green's plantation on ceder creek on the 4th inst., Mr. William Telford, in the 28th year of his age. He has left a disconsolate widow and aged father and mother, brothers and sisters....

Of a pulmonary complaint on the 27th ult.,Mrs. Eliza A., wife of Dr. Thomas Wells of this town.

Issue of September 13, 1834

Married on the 4th instant by the Rev. J. C. Keeney, Mr. Charles Thompson son of Col. Jno. Thompson, to Miss Nancy Mobly, eldest daughter of Mr. John Mobly,all of Fairfield district.

Issue of October 4, 1834

Died at her residence in this place, on Friday morning the 25th of September, Mrs. Sophia Maria Chappell, wife of Col. J. J. Chappell...aged 41 years and 19 days. (eulogy)

Issue of October 11, 1834

Died at Magnolia, Florida, on the 25th Sept., Mrs. Rebecca M'Guire, aged 44 years, leaving a husband and four children to lament her loss.

Issue of November 1, 1834

Died at his residence in Richland District, on the 20th inst., Col. Frederick Meyers, in the 70th year of his age, leaving a widow, children and friends....

Issue of November 8, 1834

Died in this town on Tuesday evening, 31st ult., Mr. Alex. Shinnie (Millwright) a native of Aberdeen, Scotland, and for the last 12 or 14 years a resident citizen of Charleston, So. Ca.

Issue of November 15, 1834

Married in Columbia, on Thursday evening, by Robt. Yates, Esq., Mr. Wm. Hennisten, to Miss Christiana Norman, both from Germany.

Issue of November 22, 1834

Married in Columbia, on the 14th inst., by the Rev. Hartwell Spain, Mr. James Agnew of Winnsborough, to Miss Eliza Ann Elliott of Columbia.

Issue of November 29, 1834

Died at Newberry, Oct. 19th, 1834, Mrs. Harriett Rebecca Johnston, wife of Dr. Burr Johnston.

At Newberry, Oct. 28th, suddenly,Major David DeWalt.

At his plantation in Kershaw District, on the night of the 20th inst., Mr. John Nelson, in the 47th year of his age...left an amiable wife.

Issue of October 17, 1835

Married in this place on Tuesday evening last, by the Rev. Dr. Leland, Dr. Charles B. Pelton, to Miss Martha M'Clure, daught of the late Dr. James M'Clure of Chester district.

AT Dr. Meacham's in Union district, on the 18th December, by the Rev. J. Jennings, Dr. C. T. Murphy, to Miss Jane E., daughter of Dr. J. Finch, dec. of Newberry district.

Issue of October 24, 1835

Married on Thursday evening the 8th inst., by the Rev. W. Q. Beatie, Mr. Samuel T. Williamson, of Darlington, to Miss Sarah A. daughter of Capt. John Terrel of Marlborough.

Issue of March 17, 1838

Married on Thursday the 15th instant, by the Rev. M. McPhersc Mr. Alfred M. Hunt, to Mrs. Martha E. Lane, all of this place.

Died at Louisville, Mississippi, on the 17th February, at acute peritonitis, Jemuel W. Brown, Esqr.,late of Union District, aged about 22 years.

Issue of July 21, 1838

Died at his residence in Lexington District, on the 10th day of July inst., Friday Arthur in the 64th year of his age.

Issue of September 1, 1838

Departed this life on Saturday morning, August 18th, Rebecca Ann, daughter of Rev. Jonathan Davis, of Fairfield District. (eulogy)

Died at his residence in Mesopotamia, Green County, Ala., Mr. Frederick Foster, late of Laurens District, South Carolina, in the 63d year of his age. (eulogy)

Issue of September 15, 1838

Married on Sunday evening last, by the Rev. Malcolm D. Fraser, Mr. William Bollinger, to Miss Catherine Carolan, both of this place.

Died on Wednesday the 18th inst., Peter Maguire, long a respectable resident of this place.

Issue of September 29, 1838

Died, on the 20th inst.,Mrs. Mary Kinsler, consort of John J. Kinsler, at their residence near Columbia. (eulogy)

Issue of March 2, 1839

Married on Tuesday 26th ult., by the Rev. William Connell, Dr. Joseph H. Morgan, to Mrs. Ann C. Pou, daughter of Martin Friday, Esq., all of Orangeburg District.

Married at New Orleans, on the 6th February last, Mr. Isaac N. Marks, of Columbia, S. C., to Miss Hannah Josephine Lee, of the former place.

Married on Tuesday evening, 26th inst.,by the Rev. G. Drehr, Mr. Drury J. Harmon to Miss Charlotte, youngest daughter of the Rev. T. Rall, all of Lexington.

Issue of April 13, 1839

Married at Columbia, S. C., on Saturday morning, the 6th inst., by the Rev. Dr. Witherspoon, Mr. Farquhar Matheson (Merchant) of Camden, S. C., to Miss Rebecca, daughter of Capt. Benjamin Haile of the latter place.

Married on Thursday evening, 11th inst., by the Rev. W. Betts, Mr. Stanmore Watson, of Edgefield to Miss Elizabeth M. Hutchinson, of this place.

Died in this place on Thursday morning the 4th inst., Mrs. Sarah Caroline Neuffer, consort of Mr. C. Neuffer, aged 26 years, 6 months and 11 days. She has left an infant child 4 weeks old-- two boys, one 2 years old, and the other 3, her husband, a father, mother, brothers and sister....

Died on the 9th inst., of a very short illness, Mrs. Robetha Longinotti, consort of Mr. Jacob Longinotti, of this place.

Died in this place on Monday the 25th March, Mr. John D. Willingham, a native of Newberry, but for the last three years, a resident of Columbia....

The following nine issues of the Telescope are at the University of North Carolina at Chapel Hill, Louis Round Wilson Library.

Issue of April 30, 1830

Married in this district on Tuesday evening last,by the Rev. Mr. Tradewell, Mr. Allen Gibson, to Miss Mary Ann Williams.

At the House of John Mason, Esq., in Chesterfield district, on Thursday evening last,by the Rev. Mr. Johnson, Mr. Stuart Perry, Merchant of Camden to Miss Elvira Wallace, daughter of the late John Wallace.

On Wednesday evening the 28th inst., by the Rev. Mr. Golding, Mr. John Preston, of Abingdon, Va., to Miss Caroline Hampton, of this place.

Issue of September 12, 1835

Married on Tuesday evening, 1st instant by the Rev. Thomas
Hall, Mr. A. W. Gibson to Miss Isabella Cason, all of Fairfield
district.

Issue of November 7, 1835

Married on Thursday evening last, by the Rev. Thos. Rawls,
Mr. Johial Anderson to Miss Emmiline A. Jones, both of Lexington
district.

Issue of January 16, 1836

Died at Maracaibo, in the State of Zulia, Columbia, about the
middle of Nov. 1835, Abraham B. Nones, Esq., aged about 42, a
native of Philadelphia--for many years Consul of the U. S. A.,
for the State of Zulia, and a respectable merchant of Maracaibo.
(eulogy)

Issue of February 13, 1836

Married on Wednesday evening the 3d instant by the Rev.C. L.
R. Boyd, Mr. Dan'l M'Cullough, to Miss Susanna M., daughter of
John M'Crory, esq., all of Fairfield district.

Issue of March 19, 1836

Died on the 13th inst., in the 63d year of his age, at his
residence in this town, Dr. Edward Fisher, a native of Virginia,
and for more than 30 years, one of the most loved and respected
citizens of oru community. The Student, in 1793, of Dr. Rush....
From the original seat of his family in Halifax (Va.) he came to
Columbia, in 1804. (eulogy)

Issue of April 16, 1836

Married on Thursday evening last, by the Rev. A. W. Leland,
D. D., Mr. Josiah E. Smith, of Columbia, So. Ca. to Miss Claudia,
daughter of the late Jas. Hibeen, Esq., of Christ Church Parish.
On Thursday evening last, by the Rev. P. J. Shand, Dr.
Alexander Moore, of Spartanburg, to Miss Elizabeth W. Taylor,
daughter of the late Col. Henry P. Taylor.
On Tuesday evening, the 5th inst., by Benj. Tradewell, Esq.,
Mr. Joseph Douglass of Richland District, to Miss Louisa Kelly,
of Fairfield District, S. C.
In Charleston, on Sunday evening, the 10th inst., by the Rev.
Mr. Brewster, Alexander Campbell, of Gainesville (Alabama) and
formerly of this place,to Miss Jacintha, eldest daughter of Mr.
Jacint Laval, of Charleston, S. C.

Issue of April 30, 1836

Married on the evening of the 19th inst., in Union District,
So. Ca., by the Rev. Mr. J. C. Keeney, Dr. A. T. Park, son of
Prof. Thomas Park, to Miss Angelina, daughter of Dr. Meacham.
In Salem, Sumter District, by the Rev. Mr. Newberry, Mr. Jack
Hardman of Montgomery, Ala., to Miss Eugenia E. Poole, of the
former place.

Issue of April 30, 1836 (contd.)

Died at his residence in the lower part of this district, on the 20th inst., very suddenly, Mr. Willis Gay. He was an industrious and honest man.

Issue of October 27, 1838

Married at Abingdon, Virginia, on the 10th of October, Col. Wade Hampton Jr. of this place, to Miss Margaret Preston, daughter of the late Gen. Francis Preston.

The following issues of the Telescope are in the Rock Hill Public Library, Rock Hill South Carolina.

Issue of December 21, 1836

Married at the residence of Mr. Drury Bynum, on Monday the 12th inst.,by the Rev. Mr. Scriver, Mr. Wm. Shiver, of this place to Miss Sarah, daughter of Mr. Drury Bynum.

On Wednesday evening last, the 14th inst.,by the Rev. Harting Cohen of Charleston, Mr. Lewis Levy, to Miss Eliza, eldest daughter of L. Polock, all of this place.

Died on Sunday the 4th inst., at his residence in Barnwell Dist., William H. Cannon, in the 27th year of his age. (eulogy)

Issue of December 31, 1836

Married in Orangeburgh District on the 21st inst., by the Rev. James H. Mellard, the Rev. John K. Morse, to Miss Caroline Ann, eldest daughter of Conald B. Jones, Esq.

Issue of January 7, 1837

Married on the 28th ult., by the Rev. John A. Kennedy, Mr. R. Dulin, of this place, to Miss Martha B., eldest daughter of Maj. Joseph Mickle, of Kershaw District.

On Sunday morning, the 1st inst.,by the Rev. Thomas Rawls, Esq., Reuben H. Fields, Esq., to Miss Eliza, youngest daughter of George Gross, Esq., all of Lexington District.

On Sunday evening, the 1st inst., by A. H. Fort, Esq., George Weissinger, Esq.,to Miss Leah, daughter of Mr. Jonathan Taylor, all of Lexington District.

On Sunday evening the first inst., by the Rev. George Halti- wanger, Mr. Jacob Hite, to Miss Elizabeth Younginer, all of Lexington district.

Departed this transitory existence in Charleston, on the 13th day of December last, Mr. Solomon Solomon, in the 52d year of his age. Mr. S. was a native of Charleston, a kind father...(eulogy)

Issue of January 21, 1837

Departed this life on the 9th inst., David Cromer, of Lexington district, S. C., aged 34 years, leaving a father, three brothers and three sisters, and numerous relatives...(eulogy)

Issue of February 4, 1837

Died in the 60th year of his age, at his residence in Clark county, Alabama, on Monday the 16th of January, Captain Jesse Summers, a native of Newberry district, S. C., whence he emigra to the above place of residence 20 years since...left an aged widow and seven adult sons....

Issue of February 25, 1837

Married in Fairfield District, near Twenty Five Mile Creek, on Thursday evening, 23d inst., by Mr. Jonathan Watts, Esq., Mr Jacob Blizard, aged 17 years, to Mrs. Wilson, aged about 75 years, relict of the late Mr. James Wilson of said district.

Married by the Rev. Burdette, on Thursday the 2nd inst., Mr James Ferguson, to Miss Elizabeth, daughter of Mr. John Ferguso residing near Beaver Dam Creek, Chester District.

Died, at the residence of his brother in Fairfield, on the 11th inst., Wilson A. Moores, Esq., of Lincoln county, Tenn.

On the 16th of January last, at his residence in Lexington district, S. C., Jacob Leapheart, aged 35.

Issue of March 18, 1837

Married in Newberry district on Thursday evening, the 9th inst., by H. K. Boyd, Esq., Mr. James Caldwell, to Miss Jane Davenport, all of Newberry District.

Died on the 4th inst., of a short but painful illness, Ophe Martha Bronson, only daughter of Mr. & Mrs. Bronson, of this pl aged 2 years, 8 months and 3 days.

Died in Winnsborough on the 5th inst., John Walter, infant son of Coln. William and Mrs. Caroline Moore, aged one year and six months.

Died on Saturday the 4th inst., Augustus Parish, at his residence in Chester District, between Fishing Creek and Catawb River. (eulogy)

Issue of March 25, 1837

Departed this life on Saturday morning the 18th instant, Dr Samuel Green, in the 70th year of his age. He was a native of Worcester, Massachusetts, but for more than forty-five years pa he has resided in this town. (long eulogy).

Issue of April 15, 1827

Married in New Orleans, 13th ult., Col. Wm. L. Lewis, of South Carolina, to Miss Letitia Floyd, eldest daughter of Gen. John Floyd, late Fovernor of Virginia.

Issue of April 22, 1827

Died of pulmonary consumption on the 1st inst., at the resi dence of Mr. Childs, Charleston, So. Ca., on his way to the Wes Indies, Mr. James M'Fie, merchant of Columbia...aged 37 years.

Issue of May 20, 1837

Married on Thursday evening last, by the Rev. Kennedy, Mr. John Cumpton, of Kentucky, to Miss Jane E. Waddell, of this pla

Issue of July 8, 1837

An old Revolutionary Officer gone. Died, at his farm, on Jackson's Creek, in Fairfield district, Captain Hugh Milling, an officer in the army of the Revolution, born at Drumbo, County Down, Ireland, on the 21st February 1752. He emigrated to America about the year 1771, and was a resident in Charleston, in the year 1774, when the first revolutionary movements was made in that city. At that time he joined a company of Grenadiers, raised by Capt. M'Call, by whom the British Arsenal was forced open...in 1778 was commissioned first Lieutenant in the sixth continental regiment of S. C., and in 1779, a Captain in the same regiment... For upwards of 40 years he was a member of the Presbyterian Church, and had the satisfaction of seeing all his children grown up and most of them become members of the same church...died on the 7th May, 1837, aged 85 years, 2 months and 16 days.

Issue of October 7, 1837

Married on Thursday evening last, by the Rev. Mr. Kennedy, Mr. Decatur L. Bronson, of this place, to Miss Mary Ann Butler, of Lexington District.

At Cokesbury, S. C., on the evening of the 29th September at the Methodist Church, by the Rev. Mr. Mitchell, Miss Margaret Ann Jones, of Columbia, to Mr. William R. Atkinson, of Georgetown.

Issue of November 18, 1837

Died on the 14th ult., at St. Albans, near Rocky Springs, Mississippi, in the 48th year of his age, William Seibels, formerly a resident of Edgefield District, South Carolina.

Departed this life on 23d Oct. last, in Chester Dist., S. C., Mr. Spencer Morison, a native of South Carolina, aged 63 years, 9 months and 22 days.

Issue of December 30, 1837

Married on the 14th inst., at Orange Grove, Sumter district, by the Right Rev. Dr. England, Wm. Rice, Esq.,of Charleston, to Caroline Margaret, eldest daughter of the late Col. Chas. Spann.

Issue of January 27, 1838

Married on the 11th inst., by the Rev. Mr. Martin, Col. J. H. Witherspoon, of Lancaster, to Mrs. McCaw, of Bolton Place, Abbeville Dist.

Died, on the 31st of December last, Theodore H. Lyons, son of Mr. Isaac Lyons, of this place.

Tribute of Respect to Dunklin Sullivan, of Perry County, Alabama, by the House of Representatives, Dec. 1, 1837.

Issue of May 26, 1838

Married on Wednesday evening last, by the Rev. Mr. McPherson, Mr. Isaac C. Morgan, to Miss Frances Bynum, all of this place.

Died at Lexington, on the 6th ultimo, Mrs. Sarah Seibels, in the 70th year of her age.

Issue of June 16, 1838

Died at Newberry Court House on the night of Sunday, the 10 instant, Mr. William A. Branthwaite, in the 33d year of his age

Issue of June 23, 1838

Married in this town, on the 9th of June, by the Rev. T. Bermingham, Mr. Owen McKiernan, to Miss Elizabeth Victoria Dupuy both of Columbia.

Issue of July 14, 1838

Married on Tuesday morning, 10th inst., by the Rev. A. Lelan D. D., Rev. Samuel Donnelly, to Mrs. Mary R., widow of the late Mr. James Ewart, both of this town.

Issue of August 4, 1838

Died on Saturday the 28th July, Mr. Joel McLemore, youngest son of the late Maj. John McLemore, of this district.

At Solitude, Fairfield District, on the 25th July, William Robert, aged one year and seven months, and son of Dr. John J. Myers.

Issue of August 11, 1838

Died on the 4th inst., at the residence of E. G. Palmer, Esq in Fairfield district, Dr. James Davis, for nearly thirty years, an eminent physician of this Town. He was born on the east shor of Maryland, but removed to this State at an early period of lif the Lunatick Asylum of this place may be said to owe its origin, its completion and its final organization to his efforts. (eulog

Died at the residence of her father in Union district, on th 28th ult.,in the 20th year of her age, Mrs. Susan Eliza Scaife, wife of Charner T. Scaife, and daughter of Mr. James Hill, leavi an affectionate husband and three small children....

Issue of November 10, 1838

Married on Tuesday evening, by the Rev. Mr. Shand, Mr. Thoma Davis, to Miss Ellen Kinsler, daughter of Mr. John Kinsler.

On Wednesday evening last, by the Rev. Gustavus Poznanski, M Benjamin Mordecai, formerly of Beaufort, S. C., to Miss Clara, second daughter of L. Polock, of this place.

Issue of December 8, 1838

Married on Tuesday the 4th inst., by the Rev. Mr. Reynolds, Mr. Francis Root, of Southington, Conn., to Miss Mary Elizabeth Heise, of Washington City, D. C.

On Wednesday evening, the 5th inst., by the Rev. Mr. Mood, Mr. Samuel Murtishaw, of this place, to Miss Ann Currell, of Fairfield District.

Married on the 22d ult., Mr. Johnathan Jones, to Miss Harriet McGarity, all of Chester District.

On the same day, Mr. Edward Steadman, to Miss Sarah Henkle, all of Chester.

Also, on Sunday, the 2d inst., by J. B. McCully, Esq., Mr. Jesse Clifton, to Miss Mary Hoey Walker, all of Chester.

Issue of January 26, 1839

Mrs. Caroline Raoul died at her residence in this place, on Wednesday evening last.

Issue of February 2, 1839

Married in Clark county, Va., on Thursday, the 17th inst., Mr. William F. Anderson of Columbia, S. C., to Miss Sidney Ann, daughter of George Knight, Esq., of the former place.

Issue of March 9, 1839

Married on Thursday evening last, by the Rev. Mr. Reynolds, Mr. William C.Reeder, to Mrs. Jane A. Oliver, all of this place.

Issue of June 22, 1839

Married at Fayettville, N. C., on the 18th inst.,by the Rev. R. W. Bailey, the Rev. Mr. E. F. Rockwell, to Miss Margaret K., daughter of George McNeille, Esquire, all of Fayetteville.

Departed this life on the 28th ult.,at the residence of her father in Mesopatamia, Alabama, in the 22d year of her age, Mrs. Angelina Park, consort of Dr. Amasa T. Park, and daughter of Dr. James Meacham, formerly of Union District, in this state.

Died on Friday, June 14th, in the sixth year of her age,Jane Rebecca, eldest daughter of Dr. James B. and Mary E. Davis, of Fairfield District.

The following issues of the Telescope are in the Virginia Historical Society, Richmond, Virginia.

Issue of July 2, 1830

Long tribute made by members of the Bar on the death of Judge Abraham Nott presiding Judge of the Court of Appeals.

Issue of July 16, 1830

Departed this life on the 28th ultimo at Darlington C. H., S. C., Mr. James H. Henry, Merchant of that place, and formerly a citizen of Lyncoln County, N. C.

Issue of July 30, 1830

Married on the 21st July, by the Rev. Mr. Boyd, Dr. William Boyd, of Chester, to Miss Charlotte, daughter of John Johnson Senr. of Wateree Creek, Fairfield district.

Departed this life, on the 3rd of July instant, at his own residence, in the district of Fairfield, Mr. David James, in the 85th year of his age...family of children and grandchildren... he was always to be found in the ranks of the Patriot soldier. Mr. James was descendant of parents, emigrants from North Briton, some years before the Revolution....

In Fairfield District, on the 16th inst., in the 19th year of her age, Mrs. Sarah Woodward, consort of Thomas A. Woodward, and daughter of Col. David Myers. (eulogy).

Issue of August 6, 1830

Died in Columbia on the 5th of July last, John Chesnut Taylo
son of John Taylor, late Governor of this state. (eulogy).

Issue of August 27, 1830

Married on the 14th instant, at the summer residence of Mrs.
Campbell, in Buncomb, N. C. by the Rev. Mr.Buist, Mitchell King
Esq. of Charleston, to Miss Margaret Campbell, youngest daughter
of McMillan Campbell, Esq., dec'd, and Henrietta Campbell, all
of the same place.
Married at Norwich, Long Island, in the morning of the 12th
inst., Mr. Townsend Dickinson, of this place, to Miss Rebecca
L. Franklin, of the former.
Died on Monday the 16th instant, at his father's residence,
in Chester district, William Jefferson Darby, in the 26th year
of his age....

Issue of September 10, 1830

Married on Thursday evening last, by the Rev. Mr. Freeman,
Mr. Thomas B. Poindexter, of Halifax Co., Va., to Miss Mary E.
Zimmerman of this place.
Died in this place, on the 6th inst.,of consumption, Corneli
Bull, aged 24, of Milford, Connecticut.

Issue of September 24, 1830

Died at the residence of her father, near Manchester, on
the 14th inst.,Mrs. Mary Rebecca McDuffie, consort of the hon.
George McDuffie, and daughter of Richard Sindleton, Esq.
Died in this district on the 2d inst., Uriah J. Goodwyn, in
the 46th year of his age.

Issue of October 15, 1830

Died at his residence in Fairfield district, on the 4th inst
of bilious fever, John T. Wrenchy in the thirty eighth year of
his age. Mr. Wrenchy removed from Kentucky to this state about
4 years since...leaves a widow....
In this place on the 14th inst., Mr. John B. Browne, a native
of Richmond, Va., and for several years a resident of this place.

Issue of October 22, 1830

Married on Tues. evening last, by the Rev. Benjamin Tradewell
Mr. Stephen C. Debruhl, to Miss Susan Cammer of this place.
In Charleston on the 13th inst.,Mr. Galloway Monteith,
merchant of this place, to Miss Mary S. Hussey, of that city.

Issue of October 29, 1830

Married on Thursday the 21st inst., by the Rev. Mr. Golding,
Col. Wm. C. Preston, to Miss Penelope L., daughter of Dr. James
Davis.

Issue of November 12, 1830

Died on the 21st of August, of dropsey, at the house of
William Adger, Esq., in Fairfield, the Rev. James Rogers in the
sixty second year of his age. After completing his education
in Scotland, Mr. Rogers was licensed to preach the Gospel, in

Ireland, his native country, at the age of twenty-one. He shortly after came to America and located in Fairfield District. (eulogy).
Died suddenly at his residence in Union district, on the 24th of October last, Mr. Spelsby Glenn, in the 67th year of his age. Mr. G. was a native of Virginia...a soldier in the American Army at the siege of Yorktown.... Shortly after the War, he emigrated to S. C. where he lived in retirement, the fond parent and affectionate husband. He has left three children....

Issue of November 24, 1830

It was with extreme regret we announce the death of Gen. David R. Williams on the 16th inst....was Governor of this state and a member of the Senate. (eulogy).

Issue of December 10, 1830

Died suddenly in this place, on the 9th inst., Capt. Manoel Antonio Esq.

Issue of February 5, 1833

Died on Friday the 11th ult., after a long and painful illness, which she bore with christian fortitude, Miss Louisa Elanor, daughter of George Jones of Spartanburgh, aged 22 years and 6 months.... her parents doted on her...left a father and mother, six brothers and two sisters.

Issue of February 19, 1833

Died on the 8th inst., at the residence of his brother near Scotch Plains, New Jersey, of consumption, Mr. Caleb Squier, one of the firm of A. C. Squier and Co. of this place.

Issue of June 18, 1833

Married on the 18th of April last, by the Rev. Wm. C. Bennet, Mr. Michael Buzzard, to Miss Mary Suber, all of Newberry District, S. C.
Departed this life, after a lingering illness, onthe 25th ult., at his residence in Alabama, Mr. John MacIver, a native of Greenock, Scotland, but for upwards of twelve years a highly respectable and much valued citizen of this town. This most worthy young man, who in middle age...a widowed mother, brothers and sisters.... (eulogy).

Issue of August 27, 1833

Tribute to the memory of Alexander Robertson Elerbe, who died at the late residence of his father, in Marlboro, the 9th of this month, aged 21 years and 5 months, after little more than 5 days illness. (eulogy).

Issue of October 1, 1833

death of Mr. Randolph who died in Philadelphia 23 May 1833, (probably John Randolph), step-son of St. George Tucker.

Issue of February 4, 1834

Married at Mount Silence, Fairfield District on the 15th
ult. by the Rev. Mr. Holmes, Edward F. Parker, Esq. to Miss
Martha W. Wiliamson (sic).

Issue of March 8, 1834

Departed this life on the 8th ult., at her father's, Col.
Chappell's house in this place, Mrs. Eugenia Calhoun, wife of
Andrew P. Calhoun, Esq. in the 22nd year of her age. She was
married only about 13 months...left a husband, and an infant
daughter, parents and relatives (eulogy).

Issue of March 29, 1834

Murereesboro (sic) Tenn. 22 February, Mrs. Betsey Trantham
died in Maury county, in this state, on the 10th of January,
1834, at the uncommonly advanced age of one hundred and fifty-
four years. She was born in Germany, and emigrated to the Britis
Colonies in America at the time the first settlement was made
in North Carolina, in the year 1710. It is a matter of history,
that the proprietors of Carolina induced a number of Palatines
from Germany to emigrate to their lands in that colony, in order
to give value to their possessions. For this purpose, ships were
prepared to convey the emigrants, and upon their arrival, the
Governor, Synte, was directed to give each 100 acres of land.
Among the number of those who emigrated at that time, which was
one hundred and twenty years ago, was Mrs. Trantham...at the
age of sixty-five bore her only child, who is now living, and
promises to reach an uncommonly advanced age. (long account).

Issue of April 19, 1834

At a meeting of the States Rights Party of Chester District,
held at the Court House on Tuesday, 1st of April...respect for
the memory of Col. James F. Woods, who expired on the 26th ult.,
Dr. John Douglas was called to the chair and Capt. John A. Bradle
appointed secretary....James F. Woods, a member of the Legislatu
of South Carolina.

Issue of January 2, 1835

Copy of a letter received in Washington City from Florida
dated November 28th 1835. Account of a duel between Capt.
Everett White, a brother of the Delegate in Congress, and Col.
A. Bellamy, late President of the Legislative Council. The
gentlemen were candidates for the County of Jefferson...Col.
Bellamy is not yet dead, but must certainly die of his wounds.
I yesterday performed the painful office of following Capt. White
to the grave....
Married in Chester district on the 17thDecember by the Rev.
Mr. Townsend, Samuel M'Alilley, Esqr., to Mrs. Mary Glenn.
On the 9th ult.,by the Rev. Josiah B. Furman, Dr. Henry H.
Clarke of Winnsboro, to Miss Louisa J. H. Goodwyn of Longtown.
Died at his residence in Newberry district on the night of
the 14th inst., after a painful illness of a weeks duration,
Jno. Henry Ruff Esq. in the 63rd year of his age. He was born
and educated immediately where he died...he has left a discon-
solate widow and eight children....

Died at his residence in Chester District, on the 16th December Dr. Uriah Jourdan, in the 36th year of his age....

Issue of November 28, 1835

Married on Thursday evening last, by the Rev. Mr. Smoke, Capt. John R. Geiger, to Miss Sarah, eldest daughter of Henry Seibles, Esq., all of Lexington district.

Marriage on Thursday the 15th ult.,by the Rev. C. L. Boyd, Mr. Alexander McDowell, to Mrs. Dorcas Hall, all of Fairfield.

On Wednesday the 18th inst., by Esq. W. Hemphill, Mr. Henry Maybin, to Miss Nancy Knighton, all of Fairfield.

On Thursday the 19th inst., by Esq. Hemphill, Mr. James W. Wall of Chester district, to Miss Elizabeth Pickett of Fairfield.

Issue of December 5, 1835

Married on Wednesday the 2d inst.,by the Rev. G. Dreher, Mr. Stephan H. Smith, merchant of this place, to Miss Margaret Dreher, of Lexington district.

Issue of December 26, 1835

Died, in Columbia, on the 3d of December, instant, Mrs. Mary E. Burnap, in the 29th year of her age.

Issue of January 7, 1831

Married on Thursday the 30th ult., by the Rev. Mr. Brearly, Jos. A. Black, Esq. of Columbia, to Miss Martha K., daughter of Col. A. F. Peay of Fairfield.

Issue of January 28, 1831

Married on the 13th inst., by the Rev. Joseph Holmes, Mr. Alex. Mooty to Miss Millicent F. Maulding of Monticello, Fairfield District.

Issue of March 11, 1831

Married on Tuesday evening, March 1st, by the Rev. Mr. Tradewell, Mr. William Griffin to Miss Eliza Wooten, all of this place.

Issue of April 15, 1831

Died in Fairfield District, on the 12th instant, Mrs. Martha Martin in the 93d year of her age.

Departed this life, on the 6th instant, in Edgefield dist., Mr. Benjamin Guignard Ioor, lately a resident of this Town.

Issue of May 20, 1831

Married by the Rev. Wm. Capers on the 12th inst., Robert Pringle Mayrant, to Francis Ann Margaret Horry, daughter of James S. Guignard of this Town.

In Camden, on Thursday the 12th inst., by the Rev. Mr. Cook, Thomas J. Wethers, Esq. former Editor of this paper, to Miss Elizabeth Boykin of Kershaw District.

TELESCOPE

Issue of May 27, 1831

Married in Camden on Tuesday the 17th inst., by the Rev. Mr.
Davis, Mr. Daniel Mandell of Washington City, D. C. to Miss
Angelina C. Mathieu, of the former place.

On Tuesday last, by the Rev. Robert Means, Mr. W. B. Means,
of Fairfield, to Miss Martha S., daughter of Mr. Jessee M. Howell
of this district.

Issue of October 4, 1831

Died of Yellow Fever, on board the Vincennes, on the 14th
September, Lieut. Paul H. Hayne, of the U. States' Navy, aged
29 years. He was buried on the evening of the same day, in
Pensacola, with the honors of war. (eulogy).

Issue of October 11, 1831

Died at his residence in this town, on the 5th inst., Mr.
Thomas Quilter, aged forty years, a native of the county of Kerry
Ireland. Industry and honesty, kindness and good nature, were
conspicuous in his character, during a residence of nearly thirteen years in Columbia.

On Thursday evening last, Mrs. Elizabeth Welsh, a native of
Ireland, and an old and respectable inhabitant of this place.

On the same day, Mr. Henry Corbet, Jeweller and Watchmaker,
a native of Scotland.

At his residence in Autauga County, Ala. on the 21st ult.,
Col. John M. Crayon, formerly of this place.

Died on Saturday last, in this place, Mrs. Harriet Couturier,
wife of Dr. Theodore Couturier, of St. John's, daughter of Mr.
Francis Marion, and grand niece of the celebrated Gen. Marion.
The untimely death of this amiable lady, at the age of eighteen,
is peculiarly to be lamented. The tears of her father now flow
for the third daughter and of her husband for the second wife,
of whom they have been bereaved in the space of two years.

THE COLUMBIA HIVE

This newspaper began as the Columbia Free Press and Hive with the issue of February 5, 1831. Later it became known as the Columbia Hive, which heading is being used for the sake of simplicity. The issues through December 29, 1832 are available at the South Caroliniana Library, either microfilm or originals.

Issue of February 5, 1831

Married on Tuesday evening, the 18th ult., by the Rev. N. W. Hodges, Dr. John D. Nicholson, to Miss Elizabeth Julia Threewits-- all of Edgefield.

In Chester District on the 27th ult., George W.Coleman, Esq., to Miss Mary Ann Kennedy, both of Chester.

Issue of February 12, 1831

Married in Fairfield District on the 3rd inst. by the Rev. Robert Means, Mr. James T. Owens to Miss Isabella Milling, daughter of Captain Hugh Milling.

In Charleston on the 3rd inst., by the Rev. C. Hanckel, William Aiken Jr., Esq., to Miss Harriet L., second daughter of Thomas Lowndes, Esq.

In the same place on Sunday evening, 6th instant, by the Rev. Paul Dean, Mr. John King Jr., to Mrs. Catharine M'Kennie.

Died at his residence near Granby on Monday evening, the 17th ult., of a short but severe illness, Mr. John W. Hayne, aged 31 years, leaving an amiable wife and eight children to bemoan their loss....

Died on Thursday the 3rd instant, about three miles from this place, of the small pox.... Mr. Clough Shelton of Union District, in the 22nd year of his age. He has left an affectionate wife to whom he has been but a few months married, and a father and several brothers....

In Charleston on the 7th instant, Mrs. Pringle, wife of John Julius.

At the Naval Hospital on the Norfolk Station, of consumption, on the 1st inst., Midshipman John C. Winans of the U. S. Navy, aged 23 years, a native of Ohio.

Issue of February 19, 1831

Married on Sunday evening, the 13th inst.,by the Rev. W. B. Johnson, Mr. Marshall Frazier to Miss Emeline Rearden, all of Edgefield Village.

Another Soldier of the Revolution has departed. Died on the 1st inst., at his plantation in Edgefield District, in the 75th year of his age, John Howard--a soldier of the Revolution; he voluntarily enrolled himself in a regiment of Continental troops belonging to Georgia, since early in 1776, in which he served three years with much credit.... He was in the battle of Stono, the siege of Savannah, August, and '96--after the conclusion of peace he visited his friends in North Carolina and returned to and settled in Edgefield District, where he has resided ever since....

Issue of March 5, 1831

Married on Thursday evening, 14th of February, by the Rev. B. Treadwell, Mr. George B. Murtishaw, to Miss Ann--daughter of Mr. Samuel Follin, all of this place.

THE COLUMBIA HIVE

Issue of March 26, 1831

Married on Thursday evening last by the Rev. Mr. Capers, Mr.
Edward Beard to Miss Caroline Rembert, all of this place.
Died in this place on Monday last, after a short illness, Mr
Michael Powers, in the 32nd year of his age. Mr. Powers was a
native of Dungarvin (sic) County, Ireland, and come to this
country about 18 months since, during which time he has been a
resident of our town....

Issue of April 2, 1831

Died in Texas, Capt. David L. Wakely, aged 32 years, formerl
of this place.

Issue of April 16, 1831

Died in Edgefield, Mr. Isham Milton, on the 16th inst., in t
71 year of his age, after lingering out many years of a diseased
old age. Mr. Milton was one of the few surviving actors in our
revolutionary struggle.

Issue of May 7, 1831

Married on Tuesday evening, the 26th ult., at the residence
Col. Butler, by the Rev. Mr. Capers, Theodorus W. Brevard, Esq.,
of this place, to Miss Caroline C. Mays of Edgefield.

Issue of May 14, 1831

Married on Tuesday evening, the 10th inst., by the Rev. Mr.
Howe, Mr. Nathaniel G. Noble of Danville, Virginia, to Miss
Amelia S., daughter of Maj. Augustus G. Nagle, of this place.
In Tennessee, Mr. Benjamin McCary, late from So. Carolina, t
Miss Eunice Cogswell, from Concord (Mass.) and late from Green-
ville, S.C.

Issue of May 21, 1831

Married on Thursday evening last by the Rev. Mr. Paulding,
Major James O'Hanlon to Miss Elizabeth, daughter of Col. David
Myers, all of this district.

Issue of May 28, 1831

Died at the residence of the late James E. Jerman, Esqr., of
St. James Parish, Santee, on Monday, the 16th instant, Mrs. Mary
E. White, consort of James J. B. White, Esqr., of Richland Distri
She was torn from the bosom of her husband and infant son.

Issue of June 4, 1831

Died in Columbia on the 27th ult., David Becket, aged 38 yea
after a lingering illness of more than a year... he eminently dis
played the affection of a husband and the tenderness of a father.

68

THE COLUMBIA HIVE

Issue of June 18, 1831

Married in Edgefield District on the 9th instant by the Rev.
N. Hodges, Major John Hughes of this place to Miss Martha, daughter
of Col. James Bones of Edgefield.

Issue of June 25, 1831

Married in Columbia (S.C.), on the 23rd instant by the Rev.
A. L. Converse, James H. Hammond, Esq., of this place, to Miss
Catherine E., daughter of the late Christopher Fitzsimons, Esq.,
of Charleston.

Issue of July 16, 1831

Death notice of Ex-President James Monroe. (Paper in black
borders).

Issue of August 13, 1831

Died in Columbia on the 7th instant of Pulmonary Consumption,
Joseph M'Clintock, Esq., aged 35 years. Mr. M'Clintock was a
native of Massachusetts, and graduate of Browns University--A
gentlemen of amiable and unassuming manners and for several years
past a respectable member of the Bar in this place.

Issue of August 27, 1831

Married on the 16th instant by the Rev. John Porter, Dr.
William Moore of Newberry to Miss Susan Caroline Gillam, daughter
of Capt. James Gillam of Abbeville District.

Issue of September 10, 1831

Died in Newberry District on the 26th of August, aged 25 years,
the Revd. John G.Schwartz, Pastor of the Lutheran Church and
Professor of Theology in the Seminary of this state. (eulogy)

Issue of October 1, 1831

Died in this town on the 5th inst., Mr. Thomas Quilter, aged
40 years, a native of the county of Kerry, Ireland...a residence
of nearly 13 years in Columbia.

Issue of October 29, 1831

Married on Thursday evening, the 20th inst., by the Rev. Dr.
Goulding, Mr. Peter Horry Ioor of Woodville, Mississippi, to Miss
Charlotte Withers Herron of this place.

Issue of November 26, 1831

Married on Tuesday evening, 15th instant, by the Rev. B. Tradewell, Mr. Burrel T. Boatright of Columbia to Miss Sophia, daughter
of Elijah and Cloe Watson of Edgefield District.
On Thursday evening last, by the Rev. Dr. Capers, Mr. Wm. Hora
to Miss Hannah S., daughter of the Rev. Robert Adams, all of this
place.

THE COLUMBIA HIVE

Issue of December 17, 1831

Married on the 8th instant by the Rev. John B. Davis, Mr.
John Poag to Miss Cynthia Miller, both in the vicinity of Louisville, South Carolina.

Issue of December 31, 1831

Lewisville, Chester district, S.
December 16th, 1833
Married on the 15th inst. by James M'Clure, Esq., Mr. Charle
Drewry to Miss Martha Thompson.
by Thomas Reid, Esq., Mr. William Crook to Miss Nancy Boyd,
of ths vicinity of Lewisville.
Mr. Landrum" Please to give the above a place in your valuable
paper. As they are all going for the union party, their names
should be in the union paper.

Issue of December 24, 1831

Married on the 21st inst., by the Rev. S. Goulding, D. D.,
Mr. Richard S. Gladney to Miss Jane A. McMillan, both of this
place.

Issue of January 7, 1832

Died on the night of the 5th inst., Mr. William Decker, a
native of New York, of a pulmonary affection.... Mr. Decker's ag
did not exceed 23 years; he was induced to leave his native home
in hopes of finding relief from his fatal malady in a southern
climate.

Issue of January 28, 1832

Married on the evening of the 24th inst.,in the Chappel at
Barhamville, by the Rev. Doctor Goulding, Dr. Elias Marks to
Mrs. Julia Pierpont Warne.
on the 19th instant by Joseph Gaston, Esq., Major James Wood
to Mrs. Harriet, relict of the late Saml. M'Creary, Esq.
on the 20th inst., by Robert Jamison, Esq., Jas. C. M'Mullar
to Miss Eleanor Davidson, all of Chester District.
In Kershaw Dist., on Thursday, the 19th last, by the Rev. Mr
Ledbetter, Mr. John S.Livingston, of this place to Miss Mary Dur
van, of the former district.
Died on the 17th January in Edgefield dist., Francis Lucinda
McLemore, daughter of Joel McLemore, aged 6 years, 3 months and
24 days.

Issue of February 4, 1832

Married on Thursday evening the 12th inst., by the Rev. R. M
Todd, Mr. Caswell Conner, to Miss Rebecca Bullock, all in the
vicinity of Cambridge.
Died at his residence near Lewisville Post Office on the eve
ing of the 12th instant after a short illness, Col. John Cherry,
aged about 50. He has left a wife and family to lament his deat
Col. C. was a man much esteemed by all who had the pleasure of
being acquainted with him.

THE COLUMBIA HIVE

Issue of February 25, 1832

Married on the 23d inst., by the Rev. Dr. Goulding, Mr. George Williams of this place to Miss Harriet Stone, of Winnsboro'.

Died in Long Town, Fairfield district, on the 15th inst., John Mickle Esq., aged 73. He has long been a faithful member of the Baptist Church, and his whole life has been one of usefulness and uprightness.

Issue of March 10, 1832

Death notice of Edwin D. Faust... At an early age he applied himself particularly to the study of Chemistry....(verse and long eulogy)

Issue of March 17, 1832

Married in this place, on Thursday evening last, by the Rev. Dr. Goulding, Mr. William E.Hughson of Camden, to Miss Mary A., daughter of the late Henry Doggett, Esq., of Charleston, S. C.

Issue of March 24, 1832

Died at his residence in Columbia, on the 20th inst., Dr. Alexander M'Dowell, in the 34 year of his age, late practioner (sic) in the neighbourhood of Flat Rock, Kershaw district.

While on a tower (sic) to Florida, Edmond S. Bacon, Esq., one of the Editors of the Edgefield Carolinian.

Issue of April 28, 1832

Died on the fifth instant in Buncombe county, North Carolina, Mrs. Elanor Mills, consort of Wm. Mills. Mrs. Mills was ninety-four years of age when she died; as a wife, mother, christian, friend was constant and sincere. (eulogy)

In this Town on Sunday last, Mr. Lemuel Carey, aged 50 years.

Issue of May 5, 1832

Married on Thursday last, by the Rev. Mr. Lyle, Mr. James Cathcart of this place, to Miss Eliza M., daughter of Maj. Henry Moore, of Fairfield.

Issue of May 12, 1832

Married on the 25th ultimo, by the Rev. Mr. Ross, Mr. Robert Purvis, of Columbia, to Miss Mary, daughter of Gen. J. B. Earle, of Pickens District.

Died on the 4th inst., Mr. Fredrick Seybt, a respectable citizen of this town, aged 64 years. His death was occasioned by an injury received in humping from a carriage with which the horses were running away.

On Saturday night (5 instant) James Holley, a youth lost his life by a fall from a horse.

71

THE COLUMBIA HIVE

Issue of May 19, 1832

Died on the 9th inst. at his residence near Columbia, Col. Henry P. Taylor, in the 47th year of his age.

On Friday last, after a painful and lingering illness, Mrs. Mary Player, daughter of Gen. Hampton, and wife of Col. Player, of Fairfield.

Issue of June 16, 1832

Married in this place on Sunday evening last, by the Rev. Dr O'Neil, Capt. William Poole, Merchant, to Miss Sarah E. Fitzsimmons, both of this place.

Died in this place on Monday last, Mr. John D. Brown, an old and respectable citizen, and for about 20 years a member of the Methodist E. Church, aged 56.

Issue of July 21, 1832

Died in Montgomery Co. Alabama on the 3 of July, Mary Ratcli and her twin infant sons, William Preston and Thomas Campbell, t wife and sons of Norborn Ratcliffe, formerly of this place.

Issue of July 28, 1832

Died in Fairfield District on Saturday the 21 inst., Mr. Mark Wooten, aged 53 years, who has been 41 years, afflicted with sev bodily infirmities; for 19 years a member of the Baptist church, and at all times a peaceable and honest man.

Issue of August 11, 1832

Married on Tuesday evening last, by the Rev. Mr. Freeman, Mr Matthew Howell Oliver, to Miss Jane Ann Nutting, both of this place.

Issue of September 1, 1832

Married in St. Peter's Church, Columbia, 20th August, by the Rev. J. F. O'Neill, Mr. Jacob Longinotti, to Mrs. Rupert B. Whit

Issue of September 23, 1832

Died on Tuesday morning, the 18th inst., Mrs. Mary Howe, wif of Rev. Professor Howe of the Theological Seminary in this place and daughter of Rev. Jedediah Bushwell, of Cornwell, Vermont, aged 24. (eulogy).

Issue of October 13, 1832

Married on Thursday evening, the 27th inst., by the Rev. R. M. Todd, Mr. Washington Williams to Miss Frances, second daughter of Mr. Vincent Griffin, all of Abbeville.

THE COLUMBIA HIVE

Issue of October 20, 1832

Married in this place on the 5th inst., by the Rev. Dr. Goulding, Mr. Levi Sherman, to Miss Elionore Charlotte Antonio, all of this place.

Died in this place, on the evening of the 14th inst., Mrs. Hannah Jones, consort of Dr. Samuel Jones, aged 42 years and six months, of a short but painful illness....(eulogy).

In this town on 16th, Mrs. Mary Cammer, consort of Mr. James Cammer, aged 62.

At the house of Mr. John Marshall, in this district, Mr. Maynard D. Richardson, Editor of the Southern Whig, of a short but painful attack of fever. In the death of Mr. Richardson who had barely attained the age of manhood, society has sustained a loss not easily repaired. (eulogy).

Issue of November 3, 1832 (two issues bear this date!)

Death of General Sumter. The venerable Patriot--the oldest heor of the Revolution in South Carolina, General Sumter is no more. He expired at his residence near Stateburg, on the 1st. (eulogy)   Chas. Patriot.

Died on the 27 April, Dr. Peter Kegne, aged 65 years. Recently in Augusta, Mr. Samuel W. Mays, late Editor of the Edgefield Carolinian, aged 27 years.

Married on the 10th ultimo, by the Rev. Mr. Terrentine, Col. W. H. Gist, to Miss Mary, daughter of Wm. and Sarah P. Rice, all of Union district.

Died on the 4th ult., at his residence in this district, Col. John Hopkins, in the 68th year of his age.

Recently in Edgefield District, Mr. Stephen Tompkins, an old and respectable citizen.

Also in the same district, Dr. Mills, of Beach Island, at a shomewhat less advanced aged.

At the Village, Eldred Simkins, jun. son of the late Col. Eldred Simkins.

Issue of November 10, 1832

Died on Saturday, the 20th ultimo, Mr. Samuel Moffatt, who had hardly reached the prime of life. (eulogy)

At Pendleton, N. C. (sic), of fever, on the 24th ult. in the prime of life, Harvey Drake of Edgefield, S. C. (long eulogy)

Issue of November 24, 1832

Married on Tuesday evening last, by the Rev. Mr. Freeman, James D. Tradewell, Esq., to Miss Elizabeth C., daughter of Mr. Jas. Boatwright, all of this place.

On the 8th inst., by the Rev. R. H. Jones, Mr. Jno. J. Sally to Miss Mary E., daughter of Mr. Stephen Moss, all of Orangeburgh district.

Died in this town on the 2d Nov., Mrs. Margaret Coleman, aged about seventy years and for the last thirty years a member of the Baptist Church.

In this place on the 11th inst., of a protracted pulmonary disease, Mr. Alexander Gallop, of the city of New-York.

73

THE COLUMBIA HIVE

Issue of December 8, 1832

Died in Madison Co., Alabama, Mrs. Elizabeth Eddins, daughter
of Saml. Landrum, aged 62 years. Mrs. Eddins was a native of
this State, and for many years a resident of Edgefield district.
(eulogy)

Issue of December 22, 1832

Married in this place on the 5th inst., by the Rev. Dr. Goulding, Mr. Wm. Jenks, to Miss Elizabeth L. Beck.

Issue of December 29, 1832

Died at St. Marks, Florida, on the 4 instant, Dr. Benjamin
F. Winn, aged about 48 years.
On the same day, at the same place, Mrs. Mary T. Blocker,
wife of John Blocker, aged 42 years--both formerly of Edgefield
District.

The following issue of the Columbia Hive is in the Gideon and
Thaddeus Welles Collection, Connecticut State Library, Hartford,
Connecticut.

Issue of November 12, 1836

Departed this life on the 11th of October, John Henry Kennedy
son of Isaac and Sarah Kennedy, of Abbeville District, aged four
years three months and twenty eight days.

THE SOUTHERN TIMES AND STATE GAZETTE

This newspaper began publication January 29, 1830. At various times it was a weekly and semi-weekly publication. The date of its demise is unknown to the compiler. All issues included here are available at the South Caroliniana Library with the exception of those from July 10, 1835-December 29, 1837, which can be seen at the Wessels Library, Newberry College, Newberry, South Carolina, and other issues with location noted.

Issue of February 8, 1830

Died in this place last night, Mr. Wm. B. Steele, a native of Ireland, and formerly attached to the Theatrical Corps.

Issue of March 1, 1830

Married in Columbia, on Thursday evening last, by Rev. Mr. Freeman, Mr. John A. Scott, of Woodville, Miss., to Miss Sarah Slann Guignard, daughter of Maj. James S. Guignard, of this place.

Issue of March 4, 1830

Married in Fairfield, on the 2nd inst., by Rev. Robert Means, Mr. David Milling, of the firm of Milling & Waddell, of this place, to Miss Jane Milling, of the former place.

Issue of March 11, 1830

Married in Columbia, on Tuesday the 9th inst., by Rev. Thomas P. Barry, Mr. Thomas Brenen, of the firm of T. & R. Brenan, to Miss Nancy A. Phillips--all of this place.

Issue of March 18, 1830

Married at Athens (Ga.) on Wednesday evening, the 17th ult., by the Rev. Alonzo Church, Dr. W. W. Waddell, to Miss Louisa M. Hilliard, all of that place.

Issue of March 29, 1830

In Darlington District, departed this life, on Tuesday the 16th inst.,Mrs. Margaret Lide, in the 19th year of her age ...left a husband and numerous connections....

Issue of April 19, 1830

Died in Columbia, on Friday the 16th inst., James T. Goodwin, Esq., aged 43 years--attorney at Law, and formerly Intendant of this Town.

Issue of April 22, 1830

Married in this district, on Tuesday evening last, by the Rev. Mr. Tradewell, Mr. Allen Gibson, to Miss Mary Ann Williams.

Issue of April 29, 1830

Married in Columbia, last evening, by the Rev. Dr. Goulding, John Preston, Esq., of Abingdon, Va., to Miss Caroline, daughter of Gen. Wade Hampton, of this place.

On the 8th inst., near Selma, Ala., Dr. Josephus D. Eckols, of Selma, to Miss Elizabeth A. A., daughter of Robt. English, Esq., formerly of this District.

Died in Columbia, on the 9th inst., Mr. William Thompson, of the firm of Thompson & Law.

Issue of May 3, 1830

Died in Columbia, on Thursday last, Mary Jane, daughter of Charles Beck, in the 7th year of her age.

Issue of May 6, 1830

Married on Tuesday evening last, by the Rev. Mr. Freeman, Mr. Robert Stanley, to Miss Emma Stone, both of this place.
In Union District, on the 20th ult.,by the Rev. Mr. Grey, Mr. John Cunningham, to Miss Amanda, daughter of Thomas Craven, Esq., all of Union District.

Issue of May 17, 1830

Died in this place on Tuesday the 11th, Miss Jacabit Polock, in the 16th year of her age, daughter of Levy Polock, merchant of this place.

Issue of May 24, 1830

Died at Col. Eldred Simkins', near Edgefield C. H. on Saturda morning last, Mrs. Susan Ann Butler, wife of Col. A. P. Butler, of Edgefield, in the 19th year of her age.

Issue of May 31, 1830

Married in this place on Thursday evening last, by the Rev. M Freeman, Mr. William Fetner, to Miss Martha Ley, both of this tow
Long obituary of Mrs. Susan Ann Butler from the Edgefield Carolinian.

Issue of June 21, 1830

Died, Col. Hon. Abraham Nott, at Winnsborough, in the 67th ye of his age.

Issue of June 24, 1830

Another Revolutionary Character gone. Died, on the 12th inst in the 74th year of his age, at his residence in Lexington Distri Mr. Gabriel Friday...served in the Revolutionary War under Sumter & Marion and for many years he has been a shining member of the Methodist Church.

Issue of July 19, 1830

Married on Thursday evening last, 18th inst., at Lonamville, near Columbia, by the Rev. Mr. Tradewell, Mr. L. Ripley, to Mrs. Elizabeth White, all of this place.

Issue of July 29, 1830

Died in Fairfield District, on the 16th inst., in the 19th ye of her age, Mrs. Sarah Woodward, consort of Thomas A. Woodward, and daughter of Col. David Myers.

THE SOUTHERN TIMES AND STATE GAZETTE

Issue of August 9, 1830

Married on Thursday the 15th ult., by the Rev. S. K. Hodges, Mr. H. W. Hilliard, to Miss Mary Beddel, step-daughter of Col. W. C. Osborn, of Harris county.

Issue of August 23, 1830

Married at Norwich, Long Island, on the morning of the 12th inst., Mr. Townsend Dickinson, of this place, to Miss Rebecca L- Franklin, of the former.

Issue of August 26, 1830

Married on the 14th inst., at the summer residence of Mrs. Campbell, in Buncombe, North Carolina, by the Rev. Mr. Buist, Mitchell King, Esq., of Charleston, to Miss Margaret, youngest daughter of Wm. Campbell, Esq., deceased.

Issue of September 2, 1830

Died in this town, on yesterday morning, Mr. John Finn, aged about 26 years, a native of Dublin, Ireland, and for some time past, a merchant of this place.

Issue of September 6, 1830

Death of Hon. Robert Stark, Secretary of State...died at his summer residence on Mill Creek, in the 66th year of his age...buried at the family burying ground in the Town of Columbia...a soldier in the Revolution.

Issue of September 20, 1830

Died at the residence of her father, near Manchester, on the 14th inst., Mrs. Mary Rebecca M'Duffie, consort of the Hon. George M'Duffie, and daughter of Richard Singleton, Esq.

Issue of October 4, 1830

Died on the 21st August last, of Dropsy, at the house of William Adger, Esq., in Fairfield, the Rev. James Rogers, in the 62nd year of his age.

Issue of October 18, 1830

Died at his residence in Fairfield District, on the 4th inst., John T. Wrenchy, in the 38th year of his age...moved from Kentucky to the State about 4 years since.

Issue of October 25, 1830

Married on Thursday evening last, by Rev. Mr. Goulding, Col. Wm. C. Preston, to Miss Penelope L., daughter of Dr. James Davis, all of this place.

Issue of November 4, 1830

Married on Tuesday evening last, by Rev. Dr. Goulding, Mr. James Martin, to Miss Leonora, youngest daughter of the late Col. Jacint Laval, of Charleston, S. C.--all of this place.

Died at Capt. Moses Dukes', on the 29th inst., Mrs. Elizabeth Donovan, wife of Mr. James Donavan, and the daughter of Capt. Moses Dukes and Mary Dukes, in the 30th year of her age.

Issue of November 8, 1830

Married on Tuesday, 26th October, by Rev. W. B. Johnson, Richard Mays, Esq.,of Edgefield, to Miss Eliza A., daughter of Dr. Williams, of Greenville District.

Issue of November 11, 1830

Died on the 21st August, at the house of Wm. Adger, in Fairfield, the Rev. James Rogers, in the 62nd year of his age. After completing his education in Scotland, was licensed to preach in Ireland, his native country, at the age of 21....

On the 4th of November last, in the 5th year of her age, at her father's residence in Fairfield District, Elizabeth Brown, 3d daughter of Capt. Samuel & Harriet Brown.

Issue of November 23, 1830

Married in Fairfield District, on the 2d of November, by the Rev. Mr. Boyd, Dr. James B. Davis, to Miss Mary E. Scott.

Issue of December 4, 1830

Married in Edgefield District, on the 25th November, by Rev. N. W. Hodges, Doct. Talbot Adams, to Miss Eliz. S., youngest daughter of Shepherd Spencer, all of the same district.

Issue of December 7, 1830

Married in this town, on the 6th inst., Mr. George L. Lyons, to Miss Eliza Coster, both of the Columbia Theatre.

Issue of December 8, 1830

Married on Thursday evening, 2nd inst., by the Rev. M. Mott, Dr. John R. Johnson, to Mrs. Mary Brown, both of this place.

Issue of December 10, 1830

Died, yesterday, in Columbia, Mr. Manuel Antonio, one of the oldest and most respectable merchants of this place....

Issue of December 18, 1830

Departed this life in the 50th year of his age, at his reside in Union District, near the Cross Keys, David Boyce...left a wife and children.

Issue of December 30, 1830

Died in this place, on Saturday evening last,the 25th inst.,
Mrs. Mary Nutting, consort of the late George Hutting, decd., in
the 45th year of her age.

Issue of January 6, 1831

Married on Thursday, the 30th ult., by the Rev. Mr. Brearly,
Mr. Joseph A. Black, of Columbia, to Miss Martha K., daughter of
Col. A. F. Peay, of Fairfield District.
ECONOMICAL MARRYING,
Married on Thursday evening, the 23d ult., by Thomas Johns Esq.,
Mr. John Hendrix, to Miss Mary Marbut; Mr. Joshua Hendrix, to Miss
Sarah Mills, and Mr. Euclidus Hogg, to Miss Kisiah Marbut, all
at the same place, and all of Newberry district. Four of the persons
married are grand children of Mrs. Sarah Marbut, who was present,
and participated in the festivities of the evening.
Died. At Toogoodoo, on Friday, the 24th inst., Franklin
Alexander Brevard Hayne, second son of William Edward Hayne, of
this City, aged 16 years and 1 month. HIs death was caused by
the accidental discharge of a Shot Gun, on the day previous....
His remains rest with those of his ancestors in the family Cemetery
at Hayne's Hall, in St. Bartholomews Parish, beside those of his
lamented grandfather, Col. Isaac Hayne.   Charleston paper.

Issue of January 10, 1831

Married in Fairfield District, on Thursday 9th ult., by James
Nelson, Esq., Mr. Wm. M'Gill, to Miss Elizabeth Hodge. On the
2d inst.,by the Rev. Jos. Holmes, Mr. Adam Hawthorn to Miss Tamer
Scott.

Issue of January 15, 1831

Married in Newberry District on Sunday 2d instant, Mr. Henry
Galman, to Mrs. Mary Count.
In Fairfield District, on the 23d ult., by Robert Durham Allen
Sharp, Esq., Mr. John Bradford, a Revolutionary pensioner to Mrs.
Bell, formerly of Gwinett county, Georgia.
On the 25th ult., by Hugh Montgomery, Esq., Mr. John Spillars
of Fairfield, to Miss Polly Freeman, late of Newberry.
Died on Monday, 10th inst., at his late residence, Sandy Run,
Lexington District, Mr. George Kaigler, aged fifty nine years. He
was an affectionate husband, kind father...left a numerous family,
relatives and friends....
On the 11th instant, William Brown, a native of Scotland, and
for twelve years a respectable citizen of this town.

Issue of January 19, 1831

Married on the 30 Dec. last, by the Rev. Thomas Ray, Mr. Zadock
Hooker, to Mrs. Mary Moorman, all of Union district.
Departed this life, on the 13th inst., at the residence of his
father, in Lexington district, the Rev. Jacob Wingard, of the
Lutheran Church, in the 28th year of his age. (eulogy)

THE SOUTHERN TIMES AND STATE GAZETTE

Issue of January 22, 1831

Married in Fairfield by the Rev. Mr. Joiner, Mr. Henry Ederi▮ ton, upewards of seventy, to Miss Lucy Newton, upwards of sixty years of age.

On the 4th ult., by Benjamin W. Richards, Esq., Mayor Lardne▮ Vanuxem, to Mary Ann Jenks, daughter of John Newbold, all of Bristol township, Bucks county, Pennsylvania.

On the 20th inst., by the Rev. G. Dreher, David Nunamaker of Lexington, to Miss Elizabeth, daughter of John Herman, of Newber▮ Dist.

Issue of January 26, 1831

Died at his residence near Granby, on Monday evening the 17t▮ instant, of a short but serious illness, Mr. John W. Hane, aged 31 years, leaving an amiable wife and eight children....(eulogy)

Issue of January 29, 1831

Married in this Town, on Tuesday last, Mr. Richard O'Neal, t▮ Miss Gracey Pearson, all of Columbia.

Issue of February 23, 1831

Married at Sandy Run, on Thursday, 17th February, by Rev. W. D. Strobel, Mr. William Assman to Miss Mary Ann Kersh, both of Lexington District.

On Wednesday 26th ult., at St. Ann's church, Brooklyn, by th▮ Rev. Mr. M'Ilvaine, Mr. George Fletcher, of New York, to Miss Mary Eliza, daughter of the late Benjamin Cornwell, Esq., of the former place.   N. Y. Jour Com.

Issue of March 19, 1831

Married on Sunday last, by the Rev. Mr. Meetze, Honirous Rid▮ Esq., to Miss Nancy, daughter of Dr. Denis Gibson, all of Lexingt▮ Dist.

Died, at his residence near Greenville on Wednesday, the 9th inst., aged forty four, Dr. Richard Harrison, in the prime of a life of most extensive usefulness. (eulogy)

Issue of March 26, 1831

Married in this town on Thursday evening last, by the Rev. Wm. Capers, Mr. Edward Beard, to Miss Caroline Rambert, all of this District.

Issue of April 9, 1831

Died on the 7th inst., in the 23d year of her age, Miss Jane Adams, of a lingering illness which she bore with truly Christian fortitude.

Issue of April 16, 1831

Died on the 5th inst., in Edgefield district, Mr. Benjamin Guignard Ioor, lately a resident of this town.

On the 2d inst., in Abbeville district, Henry Gray, Esq., a respectable Merchant of that place....

80

In Fairfield District, on the 12th instant, Mrs. Martha Martin, in the ninety-third year of her age.

Issue of April 30, 1831

Married on Tuesday evening last, at the residence of Col. Butler, by the Rev. Mr. Capers, Theodorus W. Brevard, Esq., of this place, to Miss Caroline E. Mays, of Edgefield.

Issue of May 14, 1831

Married on the evening of the 10th inst.,by the Rev. Mr. Howe, Mr. Nathaniel G. Noble, of Danville, Virginia, to Miss Amelia S., daughter of Maj. Augustus Nagel, of this place.

Issue of May 21, 1831

Married in Camden on Thursday evening, 12th inst., by the Rev. Mr. Cook, Thos J. Weathers, Esq.,of Columbia, to Miss Elizabeth Boykin, of Kershaw District.

On Thursday evening last, by the Rev. Mr. Paulding, Major James O'Hanlon, to Miss Elizabeth, daughter of Col. David Myers, all of this District.

Issue of May 28, 1831

Married in Camden on Tuesday the 17th inst., by the Rev. Mr. Davis, Mr. Daniel Mandell, of Washington City, D. C., to Miss Angelina C., Mathieu, of the former place.

On Tuesday last, by the Rev. Robert Means, Mr. W. B. Means, of Fairfield, to Miss Martha S., daughter of Mr. Jesse M. Howell, of this district.

Died at the residence of the late James E. Jerman, Esq., of St. James' Parish, Santee, on Monday the 16th inst., Mrs. Mary E. White, consort of James J. B. White, Esq., of Richland district. (eulogy)

In Philadelphia, on the 12th inst., Mrs. Rebecca Young, wife of Mr. Charles Young, formerly manager of the Theatre of this place.

Issue of May 25, 1832

Married on Thursday evening 17th inst., by the Rev. Wm. Paulding, Mr. Wm. Gaffney to Miss Charlotte J. Williams, both of this district.

Issue of December 6, 1833

Married in Charleston, S. C., on the 30th ult., by the Rev. Mr. Cobier, of St. Stephens Church, Mr. Jas. H. Reynolds, to Miss Elizabeth Putnam.

Issue of October 24, 1834

Died on the 15th inst., Mrs. Elizabeth S. Baker, aged 34 years, consort of Mr. Thomas E. Baker, of this place.

THE SOUTHERN TIMES AND STATE GAZETTE

Issue of April 17, 1835

Married at the Hills of Santee, on the evening of the 31st March, by the Rev. Mr. Converse, Robert Marion Deveaux, Esq., of St. Stephen's, to Miss Videau Marion, eldest daughter of Richard Singleton, Esq., of Claremont, Sumter district.

In Union district, on Wednesday evening, the 8th inst., by t Rev. Thomas Ray, Benj. H. Rice, Esq., to Miss Caroline Elizabeth second daughter of the late W. Wallace, Esq.

Issue of July 10, 1835

Departed this life on the sixteenth of June, at his residenc in Laurens District, Major John Black, aged 65 years, leaving a disconsolate widow and family...for a long time a ruling elder o the Presbyterian Church. (verse)

Issue of July 17, 1835

Died, at his residence in Chesterville, on Friday Morning, 26th June, after a protracted and painful illness, James Adare Sen., in the 85th year of his age. Mr. Adare was a native of Pennsylvania, and emigrated to South Carolina just before the co mencement of the American Revolution. He took an active part in the struggles of that ever memorable contest, and carried to the grave honorable scars received in the service of his country....

Issue of July 24, 1835

Married on Wednesday evening, 22nd inst., by the Rev. Wm. Capers, Mr. Peter Burton, to Miss Mary C. Camer, both residents of this place.

Died at his residence in Madison County, (Miss.), John L. Fleming, formerly Merchant of this place. He had just returned from a visit to this his native State, when he was attacked by severe billious fever, which terminated his life after an illnes of eight days.

Issue of August 28, 1835

Married, at Sumterville, on the evening of Wednesday the 5th inst., by the Rev. Mr. Furman, Charles W. Miller, Esq., to Miss Elizabeth, second daughter of Dr. J. Haynsworth.

Near Beckhamville, on Thursday evening, the 20th inst., by J J. McMullan, Esq., Mr. John Straud, to Miss Lucretia Stinson, al of Chester District.

Issue of September 4, 1835

Marriage Extraordinary. Married, in Scott county on the 8th inst., by the Rev. Mr. ------, Mr. Thomas W. Scott, a white man, to Miss Adeline J. Johnson, a mulatto girl, and reputed, or ackn ledged daughter of the Honorable Richard M. Johnson, one of the Representatives of the State of Kentucky, to the Congress of the United States. A few days after Mr. Scott became the happy hus band of the fair and lovely Adeline, he was presented by her fat the good Colonel, with a fine tract of land, known as the "Blue Spring Farm," for which a deed has been regularly made and enter on record in the office of the Clerk of the Scott county Court. The deed runs "to Thomas W. Scott and Adeline J. Scott, his wife

jointly their heirs," &c....About two years and a half ago, a Mr.
Daniel Pense married Imogena, Colonel Johnson's eldest daughter....
The laws of Kentucky forbid, under heavy penalties, a white man's
marrying a negro or mulatto, or living with one in character of
man and wife. Louisville (Ky.) Journal.
    Married on the evening of the 27th ult., by the Rev. William
Holmes, Minor Gibson, Esq., to Miss ----- Adkins, all of Fairfield
District.

Issue of September 18, 1835

    Married on Monday morning, the 24th of August, in Baltimore,
by the Rev. J. Sewell, I. Pearson Smith, M. D., of this place,
to Miss Olivia H. P., daughter of the late Jesse Levering, of
that place.
    Married, on Tuesday evening, the 1st inst., by the Rev. Thomas
Hall, Mr. A. W. Gibson, to Miss Isabella Cason, all of Fairfield.

Issue of October 2, 1835

    Died, at his residence, near Monticello, on Sunday the 13th
inst., Philip Pearson, advanced in the 90th year of his age. The
deceased was a native of Richland, but had resided near 60 years
in Fairfield. At a time when schools were almost unknown in the
country, it was the good fortune of the deceased to receive at the
hand of his father, who was a man of varied and liberal attainments,
a substantial education. In the course of a long life, he improved
upon his early advantages, and might be said with truth, to have
been a learned man...(eulogy).

Issue of October 9, 1835

    Married at Cleveland, Ohio, on the 21st ultimo, by the Rev.
E. F. Willey, Mr. John R. Cunningham, of this town to Miss Carolina
Willey, daughter of the late Newton Willey, Esq., of Boston, Mass.
    Died, in this place, on Monday morning, Oct. 5th, 1835, in
the 42d year of his age, Mr. James Ewart, after a severe illness
of less than a week. (eulogy)...an ornament of the church of which
he was an Elder. As a husband and a father....
    Died on the 14th ultimo, in Chester District, Miss Lucretia
Knox, in the 25th year of her age. The deceased has left an aged
mother, brothers, and sisters, and many other relatives and friends
....
    Died on Saturday the 3d of October instant, after a severe
illness of 14 days, George McIver Gandy, youngest son of Mrs. Mary
Gandy, of this place, aged nearly 11 years, leaving a fond mother,
and several affectionate brothers and sisters....

Issue of October 23, 1835

    Married in Union District, on Wednesday evening last, by the
Rev. Wm. Capers, Richard Sondley, Merchant of this town, to Miss
Caroline, daughter of the Hon. Wm. Rice, of Union.
    Died at Winnsboro', on Tuesday the 20th instant, Mrs. Elizabeth
Cathcart, wife of Mr. James Cathcart, Merchant, of this town.
    Departed this life, on Saturday the 10th inst., in the 33d
year of her age, Mrs. Jane Shand Bryce, wife of Mr. Robert Bryce,
of this place,and youngest daughter of the late Mr. Robert Shand,
of Charleston.

Issue of October 30, 1835

Married on Thursday morning, at the Presbyterian church, by the Rev. Dr. Leland, Rev. William B. Yates, of Charleston, to Mr Jane B. Taylor, of this town.

Died, at his residence in Fairfield District, on the 22nd inst., Thomas C. Ware, in the 40th year of his age. The decease was a member of the Presbyterian Church of Horeb, and had exerci the office of ruling Elder for the last two years. (eulogy)

Departed this life in Fairfield, the 27th inst., Mrs. Lucy F consort of John M. Waring, Esq., in the 32nd year of her age.... became a professor of the religion of Christ, in August, 1823, attaching herself to the Methodist Episcopal Church....

Issue of November 13, 1835

Married on Thursday evening, the 5th inst., by the Rev. P. J Shand, Mr. Thomas E. Baker, to Mrs. Elizabeth Gardner, all of this place.

Issue of November 20, 1835

Married on Thursday evening, the 12th inst., by the Rev. Godf Drehr, Mr. John Buff, to Miss Rachael Hook, all of Lexington Dis trict.

On last Sabbath evening, by Rev. Mr. Shand, Mr. William Graha to Miss Mary Caroline Wilson, daughter of the late Samuel Wilson all of this place.

Issue of November 24, 1835

Married on the 12th inst., by the Rev. R. S. Gladney, Mr. G. B. Nunnemaker, of Lexington, to Miss Martha Anne Coogler, of Richland District, daughter of Jacob Coogler, Esq.

Issue of November 27, 1835

Married on Thursday the 15th ult., by the Rev. C. LeRoy Boyd Mr. Alexander M'Dowell, to Mrs. Dorcas Hall, all of Fairfield District.

On Wednesday the 18th inst., by W. Hemphill, Esq., Mr. Henry Maybin to Miss Nancy Knighter, all of Fairfield.

On Thursday 19th inst., by W. Hemphill, Esq., Mr. James W. Wall to Miss Elizabeth Pickett, all of Fairfield.

Issue of December 2, 1835

Married on 19th inst., by the Rev. Mr. Nickols, Mr. James Fenton, to Mrs. M. Grant, both of Richland District.

Issue of December 8, 1835

Died on Monday morning the 7th inst., in this town, Mr. Robe Anderson Sen., after an illness of nearly two weeks. He had bee for many years, Clerk of the House of Representatives, and was i Columbia, attending to the duties of his office, when he was tak ill...funeral sermon preached in the Representatives' chamber, b the Rev. Dr. Leland.

Issue of January 15, 1836

Died in this town, on the 8th Jan. inst., Mr. Edwin Sturtevant, Musician, a native of Hartland, Vt.

Issue of February 12, 1836

Married on Wednesday evening, the 3d inst.,by the Rev. C. Leroy Boyd, Mr. Daniel M'Cullough, to Miss Susanna M., daughter of John M'Crory, Esq., all of Fairfield District.

Married on Tuesday evening last, by the Rev. Dr. Leland, Mr. Samuel Nutting, to Miss Louisa M. Price, both of this place.

Issue of March 4, 1836

Married on Thursday evening the 25th ult., by the Rev. Godfrey Drehr, Mr. Conrad Senn, to Miss Celina Hook, all of Lexington District.

In Sumter District, on Thursday the 21st of January last, by the Rev. R. W. James, Capt. John F. Haynsworth, to Miss Harriet A., daughter of Mr. Matthew Muldrow, all of Sumter.

In Sumterville, on Sunday the 21st February last,by the Rev. James DuPree, W. J. Singleton, to Miss Hortensia, daughter of the late Mr. John Haynsworth, all of Sumter District.

Issue of March 18, 1836

Died, in this town, on Sunday the 13th inst., after a lingering illness, Dr. Edward Fisher, aged about 63. Dr. Fisher was a native of Virginia and settled in this State in the year 1804. (eulogy)

In Winnsboro', on Monday the 14th instant, Sarah Jane, daughter of Robert and Nancy Cathcart, aged 3 years. (verse)

Issue of April 1, 1836

Married in Fairfield District, on the evening of the 24th ult., Mr. John Mobley Jr. of Chester, to Miss Nancy Yongue, daughter of J. L. Yongue, Esq., of Fairfield District.

Issue of April 15, 1836

Married on Tuesday evening the 5th instant, by Benjamin Tradewell, Esq., Joseph Douglass, of Richland District, to Miss Louisa Kelly, of Fairfield District.

Married in Charleston on Sunday evening the 10th inst., by the Rev. Mr. Brewster, Mr. Alexander Campbell, of Gainsville, Alabama, formerly of this place, to Miss Jacintha, eldest daughter of Mr. Jacint Laval, of Charleston.

Died on the 8th inst., at Sandy Run, Lexington District, Mrs. Sarah Saylor, wife of Esais Saylor.

Issue of April 22, 1836

Another Revolutionary Patriot is gone! Died at his residence in this District on the 11th instant, in the 80th year of his age, after a protracted illness, Major Hicks Chappell. He was a native of Brunswick county, Virginia, and emigrated when only a few years old, with his father to this State. In the year 1775, being about 18 years old, he volunteered, as a private, in an expedition against the Indians and Tories who were under the command of Fletcher, and

who were assembled in the neighborhood of 96. In 1776 he volunteered and went with Captain, afterwards Gen. Winn, to the fron-
tiers of Georgia, and there, at the surrender of Fort Barringtor
was made prisoner with the rest of the corps, and was parolled..
About the close of the war he received the appointment of Major
of the then 33d Regiment. The deceased was also elected, and se
as a member of the Legislature of this State....
    Died at Fort Barnwell, St. John's River, (E. F.), on the
night of the 1st inst., of Pleurisy and Inflamation of the Chest
Private John Rish, of Lexington, S. C., belonging to Captain
Quattlebaum's Company. He was a good solfier, and discharged hi
duty well.

Issue of May 6, 1836

    Died of Pleurisy, on the 13th ult., in Lexington District,
Mrs. Sarah, consort of Wm. C. Mitchell, aged 41 years, 7 months
and 20 days. Mrs. M. was a member of the Methodist Episcopal
Church. She has left a husband and five children....

Issue of May 13, 1836

    Married on Tuesday evening the 3d inst., by the Rev. Dr. Le
Mr. John W. Moore, of Charleston, to Miss Elizabeth, daughter of
the late David Becket, of this place.

Issue of June 3, 1836

    Married on Thursday evening 19th inst., by the Rev. Mr. Giln
Mr. James Boatwright, of Columbia, to Ellen, daughter of Charles
H. Miott, Esq. of Charleston.
    Died, in Winnsborough, Fairfield District, on the 19th inst.
Henrietta Moore, daughter of Col. Wm. Moore, aged five yeras, te
months and ten days.

Issue of June 10, 1836

    Died on the 2d inst., Jesse Lykes, one of the brave Florida
Volunteers from Lexington District.

Issue of July 29, 1836

    The Society of the Hills, in Sumter District, has been calle
to mourng a melancholy bereavement in the death of another of it
invaluable numbers. Mrs. Maria, consort of Mr. Wm. J. Rees,
departed this life, at their residence, Oakley, near Stateburg,
on the 13th May last, in the 63d year of her age. (long eulogy)

Issue of August 12, 1836

    Died at Mr. Ralls', in Lexington District on the 4th inst.,
after an illness of only a few hours, Mrs. Eliza Howell Blake,
relict of the late John H. Blake, in the 32d year of her age....

Issue of August 19, 1836

    Married on the 21st of June last, by Christopher Strong, Esq
Mr. John Connar to Miss Eliza, eldest daughter of Richard Farden
all of Chester District.

Married on Thursday the 28th ult., by the Rev. W. Flannekin,
Mr. William Wallace, to Miss Mary, youngest daughter of Charles
Erwin, all of Chester District.

Issue of , August 26, 1836

Married on the 25th ult., at Lewsville, Chester, by the Rev.
Warren Flannekin, Adam Stewart, Esq., to Miss Mary Boyd, all of
Chester District.

Died on Tuesday morning, the 23d inst., after a short and
severe illness of two days, Ann Becket, daughter of John and
Mary M'Millan, of this place, aged 4 years and 2 months.

Departed this life, at his residence in Fairfield District,
on the 21st inst., Mr. William Adger, in the 65th year of his age.

Issue of September 2, 1836

Married in the Lutheran Church at Lexington C. H., on Tuesday
evening, the 23d of August, by the Revd. E. L. Hazelius, D. D.,
the Revd. William Ernenputsch of Dhun in Germany and Rector of
the Augusta (Ga.) Academy, to Miss Eloiza Hayne, eldest daughter
of Dr. Thomas H. Simons.

Married, on the 25th ult., at Lewisville, Chester, by the Rev.
Warren Flannekin, Adam Stewart, Esq., to Miss Mary Boyd, all of
Chester District.

Died on Wednesday last, Mr. John Black, aged about 55, an
old and respectable inhabitant of this town.

Died, on Tuesday morning, the 23d inst., after a short and
severe illness of two days, Ann Becket, daughter of John and Mary
M'Millan, of this place, aged 4 years and 2 months.

Departed this life, at his residence in Fairfield District,
on the 21st inst., Mr. William Adger, in the 65th year of his age.

Died in this place on the morning of the 25th ult., of Inflammation
of the Brain, Catharine Rebecca, youngest daughter of Doyle E. and
Catharine Sweeny, aged 5 years, 8 months and four days (verse).

Issue of September 9, 1836

Died of inflamation of the lungs, on the 31st ultimo, Mr. John
Black, one of the oldest citizens of Columbia. The deceased was
a native of Manchester, England, and was born in 1781; married in
Ireland, county of Tyrone, and came to the United States in the
early part of 1811.....

Issue of September 16, 1836

Departed this life at the Shelby Springs, (Ala.), on the 24th
ult., after a few days illness, Col. Robert Dunlap, late of Newberry District, So. Ca., aged 37 years, 2 months, and 10 days.

Issue of September 23, 1836

Departed this life on the morning of the 8th inst., in the
20th year of her age, Mrs. Mary Jane Johnson, wife of Mr. James
Johnson, Merchant of this place, and eldest daughter of Mr. Whiteford
Smith of Charleston So. Ca. (long eulogy)

Died, in this town, on the 22d inst., Mrs. Caroline Herbemont,
aged 73 years. She was born in Devonshire in England.

THE SOUTHERN TIMES AND STATE GAZETTE

Issue of October 7, 1836

Revolutionary Hero Gone. Died, on the 30th ult., at 10 o'cl
A. M., at the house of Mr. Alfred Russell in Greene county, Capt
John Mayrant, an officer of the Revolutionary War, under the
gallant Paul Jones, aged upewards of 74 years. The deceased was
when quite a youth, a midshipman under the command of Paul Jones
and received a wound at the taking of the Serapis.
Died on the 22nd inst., at the residence of the Hon. Wm. Ric
in Union District, his youngest son, David J. Rice, in the 19th
year of his age. (eulogy)
                                    Lancasterville, Oct. 2, 183
Died, in this place on Thursday the 29th ult., ater an illness o
a few days, Dr. John Harrison Brown, late of Columbia--graduate
the Medical University of Baltimore...aged about twenty-three ye
(eulogy)
Died, yesterday morning, at 5 o'clock, of Billious Fever, in
the 22nd year of his age, Mr. Richard E. Hamner. This young gen
tleman had been but a short period a resident of this Town. A
Virginian by birth, born of highly respectable parentage....A
distressed mother, and several brothers and sisters bemoan him..

Issue of October 14, 1836

Married, in Sumter District, by the Rev. Mr. Baily, on Thurs
evening, the 29th ult., Mr. Samuel J. Hale, of Montgomery, Alaba
to Miss Eliza Margaret White, daughter of Mr. Joseph B. White of
Sumter District.
Died, on the 5th inst., in the 62nd year of his age, Dr. Geo
E. Smith, a native of Baltimore, but for 21 years a respectable
inhabitant of this town...member of the Methodist Church. (eulog
Died, in Athens, on the morning of the 29th ult., Rev. Samue
P. Pressley, Professor of Moral Philosophy and Belles Letters in
the University of Georgia, after a severe illness of three weeks
Died, at his residence, in St. Mathew's Parish, Orangeburg,
on the 27th ult., Mr. James S. Miles, Clerk of the House of Representatives of this State, in the 43d year of his age.

Issue of October 21, 1836

Married on Thursday the 13th inst., at the residence of Mr.
William Fulmer, near Countsville, by Esquire George M. Fulmer, M
Zachariah Day, aged 75, of Fairfield District, to Miss Martha Ba
aged 16, of Mollyhorn, Newberry District.
Married, in this District, on the 13th instant, by the Rev.
Godfrey Dreher, Mr. Joseph Gable, of Lexington, to Miss Mary
Nipper, of this District.

Issue of October 28, 1836

Died, on the 26th instant, at the residence of his father, i
Columbia, S. C., Mr. Solomon Juday Barrett, son of Judah Barrett
aged twenty-nine years.
Died, on the 10th inst., at his residence in Fairfield Distr
Mr. Elnathan Davis, in the 20th year of his age. He has left a
wife, an infant child, a mother, brothers and sisters...born and
raised in York District, but for two years previous to his death
lived in the District where he died. (long eulogy)
Another brave Soldier gone. Died, at his residence, in
Edgefield District, on the 7th instant, Mr. Stephen Cumbo, in th

77th year of his age. He was s oldier under Col. Hammond in the Revolution, and was in most of the battles of the South. He was engaged at the brilliant and successful action of Eutaw Springs; also at the Siege of Savannah....

Issue of November 11, 1836

Married in Newberry District, on Thursday evening, the 3d instant, by H. K. Boyd, Esq., Mr. William O'Connor, to Miss Sarah Coppock.
In Newberry District, on the same evening, by H. K. Boyd, Esq., Mr. David Senn, to Miss Sarah A. Hendrix, all of Newberry.
In Newberry District on Tuesday evening the 1st instant, by the Rev. Mr. Galloway, Mr. W. P. Butler, to Miss Laura Nance.
In Newberry District on Thursday evening the 3d instant, by the Rev. Mr. Galloway, Mr. Samuel Spence, to Miss Mary Hunter.
On Monday, the 31st October, Mr. James Cammer, to Mrs. Tabitha Atkinson.
Died, in Charleston, on the 8th of October, 1835, Mr. Luke Fueeny, a native of Ireland and a resident of Charleston, for the last twenty years.

Issue of November 25, 1836

Married on Tuesday evening, 15th instant, at St. Paul's Church, by the Rev. Mr. Hanckel, Dr. Charles C. Spann, of Sumter District, to Miss Mary Gertrude, daughter of Mr. John Glenn, of Charleston.
Died, at Harrisburg (Pa.), on the 9th instant, Mrs. Mary Weir, aged 71 years. She was a consistent member of the Church militant... (verse).
Died, on the 12th instant, at his residence in Marlborough District, Col. Benjamin Rogers, aged 73 years. He died after an illness of ten days, having received a mortal wound from the falling of a tree...a patriot and soldier in the revolutionary war... He has left a wife, and a large and affectionate family of children....(eulogy)

Issue of December 17, 1836

Married in Troup Co., Ga., on the 1st day of December instant, by the Rev. Mr. Harrison, Mr. George Robertson of South Carolina, to Miss Celia Calhoun of Troup County, Georgia.
Married in Sumter District on Wednesday the 23d November, by the Rev. Jas. Parsons, John M. James, Esq., to Miss Theresa C. Wilder, eldest daughter of Col. T. J. Wilder.
Married in Sumter District on the 7th inst., by the Revd. Mr. Graham, Mr. George H. Cathcart, of Winnsboro', Fairfield District, to Miss Maria L. A. Spann, daughter of the late Mr. James Spann.
Married at the residence of Drury Bynum on Monday the 12th inst., by the Rev. Mr. Scriven, Mr. Wm. Shiver, of this place, to Miss Sarah, daughter of Drury Bynum.
Died, on the 17th November, at his residence in Fairfield District, Andrew Frazier. He was a soldier of the Revolution, for which he received a pension to the close of his life.

Issue of December 23, 1836

Married on Wednesday evening, 14th inst., by the Rev. Harting Cohen, of Charleston, Mr. Lewis Levy, to Miss Eliza, eldest daughter of L. Polock, all of this place.

THE SOUTHERN TIMES AND STATE GAZETTE

Issue of January 6, 1837

Married on the 15th of December, by Wm. Hemphill, Esq., Mr. Jordon Morris to Miss Jane, daughter of Jane Gamel, all of Chester District.

Married in Chester District, on Thursday, the 15th of December by the Rev. Leroy Davis, Mr. George Egnew to Miss Jane, daughter of William White, all of said district.

Married, on the 28th of December, by the Rev. John A. Kennedy Mr. R. Dulin, of this place, to Miss Martha B., eldest daughter of Maj. Joseph Mickle, of Kershaw District.

Died, at the Lunatic Asylum, in this town, on Monday night last, Mr. Edward Cuddy, Musician.

Departed this life, on the night of the 4th of December, at the residence of Danl. D.Findley, Esq., in Fairfield District, h consort, Mrs. Rebecca Findley, in the 24th year of her age...a wife and mother (eulogy)

Died, on the 10th of December, at her residence in Fairfield District, on Pneumonai Typhoides, Mrs. Patience Freeman, in abou the 40th year of her age. (eulogy)

Issue of January 13, 1837

Departed this life in Lexington District, on the 5th instant after a protracted illness, Mrs. Anna Barbara Wise, widow of George Wise, Sr. and daughter of John Bickley of Germany. The deceased has left many to lament her departure, but their loss is her gain, for she was a firm believer in the Savior, and died in full assurance of acceptance. She was born the 7th of March, in the year of our Lord 1749, and her sponsors in baptism were Godfrey Dreher and his wife Mary Barbara. She was blessed during her matrimonial state with thirteen children, seven of whom are yet living--sixty-four grandchildren--one hundred great grand-children, and five great great grandchildren, making all of her posterity, one hundred and eighty-two souls.

Issue of January 27, 1837

Married on Thursday evening, the 19th inst., by H. K. Boyd, Mr. Samuel W. Taylor, to Miss Eliza M. Werts, all of Newberry District.

Died, in Chesterville, S. C., on the 14th November last, Mari wife of Francis Root, a native of Southington, (Con.). She has left a husband, infant daughter, and a large circle of friends...

Died, on the morning of the 4th instant at his residence, Mr. John Lowry, of Fairfield District.

Issue of February 3, 1837

Married, on the 24th January, by the Rev. Mr. Reynolds, J. M Smith, to Miss Jane E. Whitecotton, all of Richland District.

Issue of February 10, 1837

Died on the 16th of Jan. last, at his residence in Lexington Dist., S. C., Jacob Leapheart, aged 35.

THE SOUTHERN TIMES AND STATE GAZETTE

Issue of February 24, 1837

Married in Cheraw on Thursday evening the 16th inst., by the Rev. Evander McNair the Rev. G. H. W. Petrie to Miss Mary J., daughter of Mr. Lawrence Prince.

Died in Pickens Co., Alabama, on the 4th inst., after a long and painful illness of 34 days. Mr. James B. McMillan, aged 26 years, eldest son of Mr. William McMillan, of Columbia, South Carolina. (eulogy)

Issue of March 3, 1837

Married on the 19th January in Pickensville, Pickens County, Alabama, Henry Newell, Esq. of this place,to Miss Jane E. Bonner, of Fairfield District, So. Ca.

Died in Georgetown on the 13th instant, after a few days illness, Thomas R. Mitchell, formerly a member of Congress from this State.

It is also our painful duty to record the death of Mrs. M. S. M. Hardwicke, Register of Mesne Conveyance for Georgetown District, who departed this life very suddenly on the morning of Tuesday last....occupied the office of Register of Mense (sic) Conveyance of this District, for the last 12 or 14 years, and was, we believe, the only female officer in the State.

Issue of March 10, 1837

Married on the 7th inst., by the Rev. J. L. Reynolds, Mr. A. B. Williams, of this town, to Miss Sarah Louisa Jones, late of New York.

Died, at Newberry C. H. on the 22d ultimo, of influenza, Thomas Pratt, Esq.,for many years Post Master at that place, and one of their most respected and valuable citizens.

Died, in Winnsborough on the 5th instant, John Walter, infant son of Col. William and Mrs. Caroline Moore, aged on year and six months.

Tribute of Respect from the Richland Light Dragoons, on the death of Mr. James B. M'Millan of Alabama, formerly a citizen of our town....

Issue of March 24, 1837

Departed this life on Saturday morning the 18th instant, Dr. Samuel Green, in the seventieth year of his age. He was a native of Worcester, Massachusetts, but for more than forty-five years past, he has resided in this town. (eulogy)

Issue of March 31, 1837

Married in Newberry District, on Thursday evening, the 23d of March, by H. K. Boyd, Esq., P. P. Gilder, Esq.,to Miss Mary A. Toland, all of Newberry District.

On Sunday evening, the 26th inst.,by the Rev. Dr. Leland, Mr. Thomas Watt of Fairfield, to Miss Harriet M. Gandy, of this place.

On Sunday evening, the 26th inst.,by the Rev. Dr. Leland, Mr. A. H. Gladden, to Miss Mary E. Gandy, all of this place.

THE SOUTHERN TIMES AND STATE GAZETTE

Issue of April 7, 1837

Departed this life on Friday 24th ult., Mrs. Mary Monteith, in the 69th year of her age, and for thirty-three years a citizen of this place.

Issue of April 21, 1837

Died, of Pulmonary Consumption on the 1st inst., at the residence of Mr. Child, Charleston, So. Ca., on his way to the West Indies, Mr. James Mac-Fie, merchant of Columbia, after a long and lingering illness, which he bore with great patience...aged 37 years.

Issue of May 5, 1837

Died at his residence near Columbia, on the 18th ult., Mr. Ja Cougler, aged about forty-six years, laeving a wife and large family of children to lament their loss....

Issue of May 12, 1837

Married on the 7th inst., by A. H. Fort, Esq., Mr. Josiah B. S. Gregory, to Miss H. Taylor, all of Lexington District.
Died, in Sumterville, on the 2nd inst., Mr. Wm. H. Trimble, aged about 35 years. Mr. T. was a native of Pennsylvania but for the last fifteen years a respectable citizen of Sumterville.

Issue of June 2, 1837

Married in Columbia on Thursday last,by the Rev. Mr. Shand, Mr. G. M. Thompson to Mrs. Ann Sims.
Departed this life on the 24th of April at his residence in Livingston, Ala., Dr. John L. McCants in the 33rd year of his age, formerly of Fairfield, S. C. (eulogy) Voice of Sumter.

Issue of June 9, 1837

Married on Thursday evening June 1st, by the Rev. Mr. Shand, Mr. Charles B. Gibson, to Miss Augustine Eugenia Seybt, both of this place.

Issue of July 7, 1837

Married on the 21st inst., by the Rev. Donald M'Queen, Aleste Garden, Esq., to Miss Elizabeth Richardson, daughter of William Richardson, Esq., all of Sumterville, S. C.
An Old Revolutionary Officer Gone. Died, on his farm, on Jackson's Creek, in Fairfield District, Captain Hugh Milling, an officer in the army of the Revolution, born at Drumbo, County Down, Ireland, on the 21st February 1752. He emigrated to Ameri about the year 1771, and was a resident in Charleston in the yea 1774, when the first revolutionary movements was (sic) made in that city...commissioned first Lieutenant in the sixth continent regiment of South Carolina, and in 1779, a Captain in the same regiment....In his last years he was tried by many afflictions and severe dispensations of Providence, in the death of his wife one son, six daughters, following each other to the grave in rapid succession...a member of the Presbyterian Church...died 7th May 1837, aged 85 years, two months and sixteen days....

THE SOUTHERN TIMES AND STATE GAZETTE

Issue of July 14, 1837

Died in Fairfield district on the 8th inst., Jane Watt, daughter of John and Nancy Watt, in the 14th year of her age.

Issue of July 21, 1837

It is with heartfelt regret we announce the premature death by drowning, of Rev. Hugh Hawthorn, recently attached to the Barhamville Female Collegiate Institute near Columbia.... "Clarksville, (Ga.), July 12, 1837. Sometime last week, I think on the 5th, a clergyman arrived at this place in the Augusta stage, and preached in the church the same evening." ...Mr. Hawthorn, we learn, was a native of the Town of Fadney, County Down, near Banbridge, Ireland.

Issue of July 28, 1837

Departed this life in Fairfield District, S. C., on the 10th of May, 1837, and in the 32 year of her age, Mrs. Elizabeth Ashford, wife of Geo. W. Ashford, Esq., and youngest daughter of Capt. Jonathan and Mrs. Sarah Harrison. (eulogy)
Died at his residence at Summerville, near Hamburg, S. C., on the 8th inst., Dr. James Spann, aged 48 years.

Issue of August 4, 1837

Died at the residence of Maj. Seaborn, in Greenville district, on the 21st ult., Thomas Harrison, Esq., late President of the Branch of the Bank of the State, at Columbia.
At Sumterville, on the 25th ult., Mark Solomon, a native of Germany, but for many years a resident of Sumter district.
At Danville, Va., on the 24th ult., Rev. Wm. McElroy, Pastor of the Presbyterian Church, at that place, and a native of South Carolina.

Issue of August 11, 1837

Married on Thursday evening, the 3rd inst., by the Rev. John C. Hope, Major H. K. Boyd, to Miss Louisa E. Bates, all of Newberry District.
Another Revolutioner Gone. Departed this life, on the 10th of July, at his residnece in this District, after an illness of five days, Mr. Pressly Garner, in the eighty-first years of his age...a native of Virginia, and faithfully served the three concluding years of the American Revolution...lived a respected citizen of Richland District...member of the Methodist Episcopal Church.
Died, in this town, on the 5th instant, Mrs. Sophia Rees, aged 48 years.

Issue of August 18, 1837

Died, yesterday morning, Michael Harkens, a native of Ireland, but for many years an industrious and useful inhabitant of this town.
At Niagara, N. Y., on the 25th ult., David G. Coit, Esq., of Marlborough district. (eulogy)
Departed this life on the 23rd of July, at the residence of his father (Professor Adams, of Dartmouth, N. H.), Mr. Ebenezer

93

Adams Junr., late of the S. C. Female Collegiate Institute.
(eulogy) Barhamville Institute.

Issue of August 25, 1837

Died at the Grey Sulphur Springs, Virginia, Capt. George Henr
of the firm of Boyce & Co., Charleston.
Died, at her residence at Sandy Run, Lexington District, on
the 10th of this month, Mary Ann Geiger, consort of Jacob Geiger,
deceased, being about eighty-three years of age....

Issue of September 22, 1837

Married on the 7th inst., by the Rev. L. Bedenbaugh, Mr. Samu
Byers, to Miss Harriet Carolina Lester.
Married, on the 7th inst., by the Rev. B. Ogletree, Mr. L. Ju
Rodes, to Miss Elizabeth, daughter of David Hatton, Esq., all of
Newberry District.

Issue of October 6, 1837

Married at Cokesbury, Abbeville District, on the evening of
the 28th September, at the Methodist Church, by the Rev. Mr. Mit-
chell, Miss Margaret Ann Jones of Columbia, to Mr. William R.
Atkinson of Georgetown.
In Winston County, Miss. on Wednesday the 6th September, Mr.
George K. D. M'Lelland of Macon, Miss. (formerly of this place),
to Miss Margaret, daughter of Dr. James Mayrant (formerly of
Chester District.)
Married on Thursday evening the 14th inst., in the neighbor-
hood, of Beckhamsville, by D. J. Stinson, Esq., Capt. Samuel S.
McCully, to Miss Emily, second daughter of Jesse Clifton, Esq.,
all Chester folks.
Married on the 19th inst., by the Rev. L. Bedenbaugh, Mr. Joh
Sligh, to Miss Barbary Matthias, Lexington District, So. Ca.

Issue of October 13, 1837

Died on the 29th Sept., Mr. Nathaniel Monteith, aged 28 years
a respectable citizen of this place. Mr. B. was a volunteer in
Capt. Elmore's Corps, from this place, in the Florida Campaign,
where he contracted a disease of the lungs which brought him to
an untimely grave.

Issue of October 20, 1837

Died on Monday the 2nd inst.,at her father's residence in
Fairfield Dist., S. C., after a protracted illness, Mrs. Elizabet
Lightner, consort of Col. George Lightner of Richland Dis. in the
33d year of her age. (eulogy)

Issue of November 3, 1837

Married on Tuesday evening, the 31st inst.,by the Rev. Mr.
Shands, Dr. H. M. Sams, of Beaufort (S. C.) to Miss Eliza M. Blac
of this place.
Married on Sunday 8th October, at the residence of Mrs. Eliza
beth Ruff, by Rev. J. C. Hope, Mr. Christian Suber to Miss Carol
C., daughter of the late Col. Jacob Counts--all of Newberry.

Died, on Spring Hill, Ala., at the residence of Maj. John Mayrant, on Sunday last, Mrs. Mary Reese, in the 87th year of her age. She was born on James River, in Virginia, but lived eighty years of her life in Sumter District, S. C. Thus have the chariot wheels of death crushed another of the Revolutionary matrons of the Republic. (eulogy) Mobile Chronicle.

Issue of November 17, 1837

Departed this life on 23rd October last, in Chester Dist., So. Ca.,Mr. Spencer Morison, aged 63 years, 9 months, 22 days--a native of this State.

Issue of November 24, 1837

Died at Plain Hill, in Claremount County, Sumter District, S. C., on the night of the 4th inst.,Capt. Francis L. Kennedy, in the 46th year of his age. (eulogy)

Issue of December 12, 1837

Died, at the residence of Col. Wm. Moores, Winnsboro', on the 5th December inst.,Mr. John Neil, who was for many years a resident of that place.

Issue of December 29, 1837

Married on the 5th instant, by Rev. John B. Davis, James C. Hicklin, Esq., of Chester District, to Miss Rebecca, daughter of William Poag, Esq., of York District.

At the residence of Mr. John Bosh, on Thursday evening, 14th December, by Thomas Watt, Esq., Mr. Samuel Down, of Fairfield, to Miss Elizabeth Martin, of Lexington District.

Among the Passengers lost in the Steam Packet Home, was Mr. Levi Walker, Post-master of Unionville, S. C., a native of Hartford, Connecticut. Mr. W. emigrated to this State several years ago, and subsequently came three of his brothers. About two years since, one of them died at St. Augustine whither he had gone in search of health; another died last spring at Union Court House, of a pulmonary consumption; a third was lost in the summer on board of the schooner S. S. Mills, bound from St. Augustine for Charleston, and the subject of this notice, in the Home. Mr. W. had resided for several years at Unionville, where he has left a wife and child.

Issue of January 5, 1838

Married, on 12th December, by the Rev. Mr. M'Pherson, Dr. Thomas W. Briggs, to Miss Sarah A., only daughter of Mr. Richard Ragin, both of Clarendon, Sumter district.

On the 29th November, by the Rev. S. Davis, Mr. T. D. Coffee, to Miss E. L., second daughter of the late David Robinson, dec'd, all of Orangeburg.

At Tuscaloosa, Ala., on Friday the 8th December, by the Rev. James A. Butler, Mr. Thomas J. Butler, of Mobile, formerly of this place, to Miss Helen N., daughter of the late Joshua Leavens, of Mobile, Ala.

THE SOUTHERN TIMES AND STATE GAZETTE

Issue of February 9, 1838

Married, in this place, on the 6th inst., by the Rev. Malcom McPherson, Mr. Leslie Smyth, of Aberdeen, Scotland, to Miss Ann Matilda O'Hanlon, daughter of T. O'Hanlon, Esq., of Columbia.

Issue of February 16, 1838

Married on Thursday evening, the 8th inst., by the Rev. L. Bedenbaugh, Mr. Elijah Elmore, of Newberry, to Mess Celia, daughter of Jacob Rall, of Lexington District.

On Thursday the 8th inst., by the Rev. Godfrey Dreher, Jesse Coogler, Esq., P. M. at Oakville, Lexington district, to Miss Spartha Meetze, of Georgia.

Issue of February 23, 1838

Married on the 15th inst., by the Rev. Mr. Boyd, Mr. Robert Sloan to Miss Susannah McDowell, daughter of John McDowell, all of Fairfield District.

Died in Cheraw, on Monday evening last, of a lingering illness John Middleton, Esq., one of the Representatives of Chesterfield District, in the State Legislature.

Issue of March 2, 1838

Died, in this place, on the 23d ult., Mrs. Esther Waddell, aged 80 years. Mrs. Waddell was a native of the county of Donegal in Ireland. She emigrated to this place in 1830, and has since resided in great cheerfulness and comfort with her son Robert. She became a member of the Seceder Church at the age of 18....

Departed this life on the 20th ult., Mrs. Mary Ewart, in the 76th year of her age. This aged servant of God was born in the county Down, Ireland, and came to this country a few years ago in company with her youngest child and only daughter....

Issue of August 17, 1838

Died on the 4th inst., at the residence of E. G. Palmer, in Fairfield district, Dr. James Davis, for nearly thirty years an eminent physician of this Town. He was born on the east shore of Maryland, but removed to this State at an early period of life. (long eulogy) <u>Telescope</u>.

Died, at Camden, on the 3rd inst., Dr. Thomas Abbott, of Long town, Fairfield district.

Abbott, Thomas 96
Abney, Joel 30
Acy, Dan'l. 38
Adams, Dr. 44
    Ebenezer Jr. 93, 94
    Hannah S. 69
    James 10
    Jane 80
    John 25, 52
    Laura 44
    Rev. Mr. 48
    Robert 19, 69
    Sarah 52
    Talbot 78
Adamson, Amelia 30
    Elizabeth 5
    John 5, 30
Adare, James 82
Adger, William 35, 62, 78, 87(2)
Adkins, Miss _____ 83
Aertsen, Guilliam 11
Agnew, James 54
Aiken, William Jr. 67
Allen, Charles 9
Alston, Joseph 32
    Samuel 53
Ancrum, William 13
Anderson, Johial 56
    Robert 84
    William F. 61
    W. W. 50
Antonio, Elinore Charlotte 73
    Emanuel 9
    Manoel 63
    Manuel 78
Appling, William 8
Arkwright, Richard 1
Arthur, Friday 54
    Jesse 15
    Julia 13
    Susan 15
Asbury, Francis 31
Ashford, Elizabeth 93
    Geo. W. 93
Assman, William 80
Atkinson, Tabitha 89
    William R. 59
Atwood, C. B. 44

Bacon, Edmond S. 71
    Edmund 35
Bailey, Mary 47
    R. W. 61
    Thomas 47
Baily, Rev. Mr. 88
Baker, Elizabeth S. 81
    Harriott 4
    J. 4
    Thomas E. 81, 84
    Wm. 44

Baldrich, Thomas 3
Baldwin, David 12
Ball, Martha 88
Barber, Comfort Ann 45
    Nath'l. 45
Barker, Mr. _____ 8
Barkley, Thomas 48
Barns, Albert 22
    Madaline 25
Barnwell, John 10
    Mary Huston 10
Barrett, Judah 88
    Michael 8
    Solomon Juday 88
Barrillon, Christopher 19
Barry, Commodore 6
    Rev. Mr. 50
    Thomas P. 75
Barton, Benjamin Smith 29
    George 5
Bates, John 35
    Louisa E. 93
Bay, Martha Davis 17, 42
    Sarah H. H. 25
    William 33
Beard, Edward 68, 80
    James 2
    Joshua 27
    Thomas 27
    William 19
Beatie, W. Q. 54
Beck, Charles 76
    Elizabeth L. 74
    Mary Jane 76
Becket, David 68, 86
    Elizabeth 86
Beddel, Mary 77
Bedenbaugh, Rev. L. 94(2), 96
Beeket, David 33
    Nancy 32
Bell, Mrs. _____ 79
    Robert 46
Bellamy, Capt. A. 64
Belshre, W. 39
Belton, Jonathan 7
    William A. A. 35
Bennet, William C. 49, 63
Benson, Abner 45
    Elizabeth D. 45
    Mary 12
    William 3
Bermingham, T. 60
Bernhard, Rev. Mr. 11
Berry, Rebecca H. 32
Betts, W. 55
Bickley, Jacob 10
    John 90
Billings, Andrew 37
Birge, William 16

Black, Eliza M. 94
    Frances A. E. 53
    James 53
    John 16, 42, 82, 87(2)
    John W. 42
    John Wentworth 16
    Jos. A. 65
    Joseph A. 79
Blackburn, Eliza 37
    Georgianna Va. 34
    Professor 34
Blake, Eliza Howell 86
    John H. 86
Blanding, Abraham 29
Blizard, Jacob 58
Blocker, Abner 11, 26
    Amelia 26
    John 74
    Mary T. 74
Boatner, Mary 25
Boatright, Burrel T. 69
    Mary 32
Boatwright, Elizabeth C. 73
    Jas. 73
Bobo, Barram 47
    Sarah 37
Bollinger, William 55
Bomar, Thomas 13
Bonaparte, Jerome 7
Bond, Rebecca 16
Bones, James 69
    Martha 69
Bonhan, Elizabeth J. 42
Bonner, Jane E. 91
Bonsall, Sermon 44
Bookman, Jacob 53
Boothe, Benjamin W. 22
Bosh, John 95
Bourne, Jane 22
Bow, John 37, 47
Bowen, Bishop 13, 39
Bowie, Benjamin 38
    Hollan 38
    John 17
Bowhillon, Joseph L. 39
Boyce, David 78
Boyd, C. L. 56, 65
    C. LeRoy 84, 85
    H. K. 58, 89(2), 90, 91, 93
    M. 46, 48
    Mary 87(2)
    Nancy 70
    Nathan 34
    Rev. Mr. 61, 78, 96
    William 61
Boykin, Elizabeth 65, 81
Boyles, Martha 25
Bradbury, William F. 28
Bradford, Andrew 48
    John 79
Bradley, John A. 64
Braieley, Rev. Mr. 45, 48
Branthwaite, E. F. 52

Branthwaite cont.
    William A. 60
Brearly, Rev. Mr. 65, 79
Bremar, Peter 24
    Sarah 24
Brenan, Charles 15
    Daniel 33
    Thomas 75
Brennan, Ann 49
    Thomas 49
Brevard, Caroline Ann 20
    Eugene Joseph 52
    Joseph 14, 40
    Theodorus W. 20, 68, 81
Brewster, Rev. Mr. 56, 85
Brickell, Susan M. 23
    William A. 23
Briggs, Catharine 35
    Mary 23
    Sarah 21
    Thomas W. 95
    William 15, 21, 23(2),
        35, 41
Britt, Ann 15
Brock, John Jr. 1
Bronson, Decatur L. 59
    Francis S. 50
    Mr. & Mrs. 58
    Ophelia Martha 58
Broselmann, Thomas J. 52
Brown, Barnet H. 33
    Daniel 33
    Elizabeth 78
    Harriet 78
    Jemuel W. 54
    John 5
    John D. 20, 72
    John Harrison 88
    Lydia M. 15, 41
    Margaret 48
    Mary 78
    Richard 5
    Samuel 78
    William 79
Browne, John B. 62
Bruce, John 12(2)
    Mary 12
Bryant, David 30
Bryce, Jane Shand 83
    Robert 83
Buck, Rev. Mr. 22
Buff, John 84
Buist, Rev. Mr. 62, 77
Bull, Cornelius 62
Bullock, Rebecca 70
Bundrick, John 24
Burchmore, Rebecca 32
Burdette, Rev. 58
Burgoyne, Lt. Gen. 1
Burnap, Mary E. 65
Burnet, James 22
Burton, Peter 82
Busby, T. 51

Bushwell, Jedehiah 72
Butler, A. P. 76
  Capt. 68
  Col. 81
  Frank 36
  Gen. 51
  Harriet Hayne 53
  James A. 95
  Judge 53
  Louisa 36
  Mary Ann 59
  Susan Ann 76(2)
  Thomas J. 95
  W. P. 89
Buyck, Bernadus 7
Buzzard, Michael 63
Byers, Samuel 94
Bynum, Drury 57, 89
  Frances 59
  Sarah 57, 89
Byrd, R. 5
Byrne, Roger 8

Cabeen, Alex'r. 12
Cadwallader, Mary 43
Caldwell, James 9, 58
  John 29
  Mrs. 29
Calhoun, Andrew P. 52, 64
  Celia 89
  Eugenia 52, 64
  Patrick 2
Calver, Rebecca 2
Calvert, John 2, 6
Camer, Mary C. 82
Cammer, James 73, 89
  Mary 73
  Susan 62
Campbell, Alexander 56, 85
  Henrietta 62
  Margaret 62, 77
  McMillan 62
  Mitchell 62
  Mrs. 62, 77
  Rev. Mr. 23, 44
  Wm. 77
Cannon, Eliza 33
  Samuel 19
  Sarah 19
  William H. 57
Cantey, Ann V. 31
  John 5
  Polly 5
Canty, Susan Flud 9
Capers, John 33
  Rev. Dr. 69
  Rev. M. 68, 81
  Rev. Mr. 12, 68, 83
  William 33, 65, 80, 82
Carey, Lemuel 71
Carney, John 30
Carolan, Catherine 55
Carr, Mary 20

Carroll, Charles R. 43
  Chs. 5
  Miss. 5
  Bishop 5
Carter, Ann 41
  John 23
Carwile, John S. 39
  Stephen W. 39
Casey, Ann 30
  James 30
Cason, Isabella 56, 83
Cathcart, Elizabeth 83
  George H. 89
  James 71, 83
  Nancy 85
  Robert 85
  Sarah Jane 85
Cater, Richard B. 16
Cato, Wm. 13
Caughman, Rebecca 48
  West 48
Ceason, Elizabeth G. 36
  Josiah 36
Champlain, William 24
Champy, Mary Ann Eleonora 9
Chaplain, Silas 7
Chapman, Esther 31
  Giles 12, 31
Chappell, Col. 52, 64
  Hicks 85
  J. J. 53
  Rebecca C. 53
  Sophia Marie 53
Charlton, John K. M. 20
Chenault, Marie A. 27
Cherry, John 70
Child, Mr. 92
Childs, Mr. 58
Chisolm, Alexander 10
Church, Alonzo 75
Clark, Caleb 48
  James L. 17, 42
  Robert 7
Clarke, Henry H. 64
Clendiner, Robert 26
Cleves, John 24
Clifton, Algernon S. 20
  Claiborn 38
  Emily 94
  Jesse 60, 94
  Rev. Mr. 25, 27, 38
Clissey, Peter 42
Coalter, David 27
Coate, Betsy 11
  Henry 11
Coates, John 48
Cobier, Rev. Mr. 81
Coe, L. H. 46
Coffee, T. D. 95
Coffin, Ebenezer 14
  Robert S. 14
Cogswell, Eunice 68
Cohen, Harting 57, 89

Coit, David G. 93
Coleman, George W. 67
  Margaret 73
  Mrs. 21
  Wm. 21
Compty, Charles 10
  John 4
  Mrs. 4
Connar, John 86
Connell, William 55
Conner, Caswell 70
Converse, A. L. 69
  Rev. Mr. 45, 50, 82
Conyers, J. 30
Coogler, Jacob 84
  Jesse 96
  Martha Ann 84
Cook, Rev. Mr. 65, 81
Copeland, Joseph T. 52
Coppock, Sarah 89
Corben, Samuel P. 13, 40
Corbet, Henry 66
Cornwell, Benjamin 80
  Mary Eliza 80
Coryell, Jesse 30
Coster, Eliza 78
Cougler, Jacob 92
Count, Mary 79
Counts, Caroline C. 94
  Jacob 94
Countz, Jacob 39
Couturier, Harriet 66
  Theodore 66
Cox, Thomas Campbell 8
Crafts, William 38
Crane, Alexander 52
Craven, Amanda 76
  Thomas 76
Crayon, John M. 66
Creyon, Catherine 14, 40
Crockett, Robert M. 35
Cromer, David 57
Crook, William 70
Crowther, James 47
Crumpton, Alexander 44
Crymes, Henry 8
Cuddy, Edward 90
Cully, John W. 50
Cumbo, Stephen 88
Cumpton, John 58
Cunningham, John 76
  John R. 83
Cureton, Thomas T. 15
Currell, Ann 60

Dalcho, Rev. Dr. 43
Dale, Mary 8
  Robert 8
Dallot, Francis 27
Daniel, Asenith 13
  Elisha 16
  James 14, 40
  Jose 4

Daniel cont.
  Mary 19
Darby, William Jefferson 62
Davenport, Jane 58
Davidson, Eleanor 70
Davis, Drury 27
  Elnathan 88
  Henry W. 17
  James 60, 62, 77, 96
  James B. 61, 78
  Jane Rebecca 61
  John B. 70, 95
  John R. 48
  Jonathan 54
  Leroy 90
  Mary E. 61
  Mr. _____ 46
  Penelope L. 62, 77
  Rebecca Ann 54
  Rev. Mr. 20, 66, 81
  Rev. S. 95
  Sidney M. 37
  Thomas 60
Dawkins, Elijah 45
Day, Zachariah 88
Dean, Paul 67
Dearborn, Henry 24
DeBruhl, Harriet Louisa 21
  Jesse 21
  Stephen C. 62
Decker, William 70
DeGraffenried, Trezvant 19
Delahunt, Robert 26
De La Mar, Francis 29
Delane, Ann W. 32
  Peter L. 29
Deleon, Jacob 22
Delesseline, Francis H. 30
Dennis, Richard Jr. 8
Desaussure, Caroline 29
  Judge 29, 39
Deveaux, Robert Marion 82
Develin, William 18, 43
De Walt, David 54
Dexter, Samuel 32
Dickinson, Townsend 62, 77
Dickson, Michael 34
Dimon, Jane Adelaide 50
Dinkins, Eliza 14, 40
  Elizabeth 42
  Elizabeth C. 17
  Thomas 10
Doan, Stephen W. 38
Doggett, Henry 71
  Mary A. 71
Donaldson, John 48
Donnelly, Samuel 60
Donovan, Elizabeth 78
  James 78
Douglas, James 2
  John 64
Douglass, Joseph 56, 85
Down, Samuel 95

Dozier, Abraim Giles 6, 31
  Elizabeth Giles 6
Drake, Harvey 73
Dreher, G. 80
  Godfrey 88, 90, 96
  John R. 48
  Mary Barbara 90
Drehr, G. 55, 65
  Godfrey 84, 85
  Margaret 65
Drenon, Jane 30
Drewry, Charles 70
Duckett, Jacob 47
  Sarah 47
Dudley, Jane E. 18
Duke, G. 48
Dukes, Mary 78
  Moses 78
Dulin, R. 90
Duncan, Louisa C. 33
Dunlap, David E. 8, 9
  Rev. Mr. 2, 3, 4, 5, 6, 7
  Robert 87
  Susanna 8
Dunlapp, John 34
Dunovan, Mary 70
Dunn, Jno. M. 36
  Wm. M. 36
Dunwoody, Rev. Mr. 25
  Samuel 25
Du Pree, James 85
Dupuy, Elizabeth V. 60
Duyckinch, Benjamin 13

Earle, Elias 29, 46
  Francis W. 29
  J. B. 71
  Mary 71
  Samuel 51
Eckols, Josephus D. 75
Eddens, Elizabeth 74
Ederington, Henry 80
Edwards, John 33
  Mary 33
  Mohala 48
Egleburger, Louisa 48
Egnew, George 90
Eigleberger, George 45
Elerbe, Alexander Robertson 63
Elliott, Eliza Ann 59
Ellis, _____ 25
Ellison, Elizabeth 45
  Peggy 24
  William 45
Elmore, Elijah 96
  F. H. 14, 40
Emmet, Thomas Addis 18
England, Bishop 43
  Joannah 43
  Rev. Dr. 59
English, Bond 50, 52
  Elizabeth A. A. 75
  Rev. Mr. 49, 50

English cont.
  Robert 75
Ennis, William 36
Ernenputsch, William 87
Erwin, Charles 87
  Mary 87
Ethridge, Susannah 31
Evans, Charles 29
  David 3
  David R. 4
  Elizabeth 37
  Joseph 26
  Margaret 26
  Richard 26
  T. 30
Ewart, David 25, 32, 35
  James 60, 83
  Mary 96
  Mary R. 60
  Samuel 18

Faber, Ephraim 49
Fair, Edmund 31
Farden, Eliza 86
  Richard 86
Farmir, Lewis 25
Farrow, Elizabeth 43
Faust, Daniel 50, 51
  Edwin D. 71
  Jacob J. 18
  Jane Arabella 51
  J. J. 43
  John 5
  Mary C. 50
Felder, Eliza M. 43
  Lewis 18
Feller, John 1
Fenton, James 16, 84
Ferguson, Elizabeth 58
  James 58
  John 58
Fetner, William 76
Fields, Reuben H. 57
Finch, David 51
  Dr. 29
  Dr. J. 54
  Jane E. 54
  Mrs. 51
Findley, Danl. D. 90
  Rebecca 90
Finley, Elizabeth 13
Finn, John 77
Fishburn, Francis B. 43
  Sarah F. 43
Fisher, Edward 56, 85
Fitz, George 36
Fitzgerald, Henry Thomas 27
Fitzsimons, Catherine E. 69
  Christopher 69
  Paul 14, 40
  Sarah E. 72
Flanagan, Reuben 41
Flannekin, W. 87(2)

Fleming, David 5
  John L. 82
Fletcher, George 80
Flinn, Henrietta Ellen 34
  Thomas J. 34
Flowers, William 41
Floyd, Letitia 58
  John 58
Folker, Patrick 14, 15
  P. H. 17(2)
  Rev. Mr. 14(2), 15, 16, 17(2),
    18, 19, 21, 35, 37, 40(2),
    41, 42(2)
Follin, Ann 67
  Samuel 67
Ford, Elias 32
Fort, A. A. 57, 92
  Isaac 48
Foster, Frederick 54
  James 6
Fouts, Elizabeth Ann 53
Fox, James A. 15
  John 48
Franklin, Rebecca L. 62, 77
Frazer, Caroline A. 29, 33
  James 29, 33
  Malcolm D. 55
Frazier, Andrew 89
  Isaac 24, 45
  Marshall 67
Free, George 47
  Nancy 47
Freeman, Patience 90
  Polly 79
  Rev. Mr. 48, 62, 72, 73, 75,
    76(2)
Freshley, Mr. 26
Friday, Gabriel 76
  Martin 55
Fueeny, Luke 89
Fulmer, _____ 51
  George M. 88
  William 88
Furman, Josiah B. 64
  Rev. Dr. 25, 82
Furney, Wm. H. 30

Gable, Joseph 88
Gadsden, Rev. Dr. 13, 40
Gaffney, Wm. 81
Gaillard, Octavia 13
  Theodore 13
Gaire, Hugh 10
Gales, Thomas 29
Gallop, Alexander 73
Galloway, Rev. Mr. 89(2)
Galman, Henry 79
Gamel, June 90
Gandy, George McIver 83
  Harriet M. 91
  Mary 83
  Mary E. 91
Garden, Alester 92

Gardiner, M. F. 39
Gardner, Elizabeth 84
  Henry 19
Garlington, Edwin 43
  Elenor 43
Garner, Pressly 93
Garrett, Stephen 34
Gaston, Joseph 70
Gay, Willis 57
Geddes, John Jr. 19
Geiger, Ann E. 17, 42
  Catherine 3
  Henry 47
  Jacob 3, 94
  John R. 65
  Major 2
  Mary Ann 94
George, Enoch 21
Gerald, Thomas 2
Geyer, Peter 7
Gibbes, Alston 13
  C. E. 52
  Robert W. 18, 52
  Samuel Wilson 52
Gibson, Allen 55, 75
  A. W. 56, 83
  Charles B. 92
  Denis 80
  Minor 83
  Nancy 80
  Stephen 51
Gilder, P. P. 91
Giles, Mary 41
Gillam, James 69
  Susan Catherine 69
Gillon, Alexander 7
Gilman, Rev. Mr. 86
Gist, Wm. F. 39
  W. H. 73
Gladden, A. H. 91
Gladney, Richard S. 70
  R. S. 84
Glenn, John 89
  Mary 47, 64
  Mary Gertude 89
  Spelsby 63
  William C. 14, 40
Glimp, Elizabeth 49
Glover, John 41
Golding, Rev. Mr. 55, 62
Gooch, John 52
Goodman, Duke 10
  Walter 36
Goodwin, James T. 75
  Martha 32
Goodwyn, Francis 10
  James 34
  Jesse H. 17, 43
  John 3
  Louisa J. H. 64
  Sarah 10
  Silvia P. 10
  Uriah J. 62

Goodwyn cont.
  William 3, 10
Goolrick, Doyle S. 42
Gore, James 24
Gourdin, Theodore 35
Goulding, Rev. Dr. 69, 70, 71(2),
    73, 74, 75, 77, 78
  Rev. S. 70
Grafton, Eliza 16
Graham, Joel 34
  Rev. Mr. 89
  William 84
Grant, Mrs. M. 84
Gray, Benjamin 3
  Henry 80
  John 16
  Mary G. 16
Gregg, Mary Virginia 52
  William 52
Gregory, Josiah B. S. 92
Green, Allen Jones 20, 43
  F. W. 21
  Samuel 53, 58, 91
  Thomas 35
Greenwood, Caroline M. 15, 41
Greer, Thos. 37
Grey, Rev. Mr. 76
Griffin, Frances 72
  Vincent 72
  William 65
Gross, Eliza 57
  George 57
Guignard, Caroline E. 18
  Eliza Saunders 23, 45
  James S. 18, 24, 45, 65, 75
  Sarah Slann 75
Gunthrop, John 49
Gutsell, Richard 41

Haile, Benjamin 55
  Elizabeth 55
  William 15
Hails, Eleanor 3
  Mary 18
  Robert 31
Hale, Samuel J. 88
Hall, Alexander 4
  Daniel 41
  Dorcas 65, 84
  Thomas 56, 83
  William 20
Haltiwanger, George 57
Hamilton, A. C. 39
  Delphia Adelia 39
Hamiter, John 49
Hampton, Alfred 39
  Ann 48
  Caroline 55, 75
  Gen. 72
  Harriet 38
  Henry 37
  Richard 1
  Wade 5, 38, 48, 75

Hampton cont.
  Wade Jr. 57
Hammond, Col. 89
  Elisha 11, 46
  James H. 69
Hamner, Richard E. 88
Hanckel, C. 67
  Rev. Mr. 89
Hanckell, Rev. Mr. 43
Hanckle, Rev. Mr. 25
Hane, Henry 7
  John W. 80
  John Wolfe 25
  Nicholas 17, 44
Hankle, Rev. Mr. 27
Hannah, Arch. 46
  James 32
  Nancy 32
Hardman, Jack 56
Hardwicke, M. S. M. 91
Hardt, Peter 25
Harkins, Michael 93
Harman, Jacob 48
Harmon, Drury J. 55
  John 22
  Noah Simpson 22
Harper, Robert Goodloe 5
  Rev. Mr. 9
Harrington, Elizabeth F. 44
  Spencer C. 47
  Y. J. 44
Harris, B. J. 42
  Edward 19
  Mary Ann 42
  Minyard 5
Harrison, Burr 4
  Elizabeth H. 25
  Jonathan 93
  Rev. Mr. 89
  Richard 31, 46, 80
  Sarah 93
  Sophia 4
  Thomas 93
Harson, Mary 50
Hart, B. 48
  Mary 48
  Rev. Mr. 44
Hatton, David 94
  Elizabeth 94
Havis, Jesse 16
Hawkins, Benjamin 32
  Joseph 16
Hawthorn, Adam 79
  Hugh 93
Hay, William Howell 34
Hayne, Eloiza 87
Franklin, Alex. Brevard 79
  Isaac 79
  John W. 67
  Paul H. 66
  William Edward 79
Haynesworth, Elizabeth 82
  Hortensia 85

103

Haynesworth cont.
James 46, 82
John 85
John F. 85
Susan C. 46
Haywood, John 18
Hazelius, E. L. 87
Heartwell, Jesse 46
Heath, Ethiel 2
Rebecca 52
Thomas 2
Thos. Jr. 21
W. 52
Hemphill, W. 65, 84(2)
Wm. 48, 90
Henderson, David 11
Hannah S. 32
John 29
Hendrick, Louisa Marie 33
Mary 3
Robert 3
Hendrix, John 79
Joshua 79
Mary 34
Sarah A. 89
Henkle, Sarah 60
Henley, Robert 22
Hennisten, Wm. 54
Hennon, Rebecca 21
Henry, George 94
James H. 61
Prof. 14
T. C. 17
Henson, Martha 48
Herbemont, Alexander 17, 42
Caroline 87
Herman, Elizabeth 80
John 80
Herndon, Berry 46
Lucy B. 46
Herron, Charlotte Withers 69
Herrons, Susannah 46
Wm. 46
Hibeen, Claudia 56
Jas. 56
Hicklin, James C. 95
Hightower, Kittey 5
Hill, James 60
Rebecca C. 19
Hilleary, Eliza A. 18, 43
William 18, 43
Hillegas, George A. 17
Hilliard, H. W. 77
Louisa M. 75
Hilliary, Martha 38
Thomas 38
William 38
Hirons, Ann Wood 11
Hite, Jacob 57
Hodge, Elizabeth 79
Hodges, Col. 49
Prudence 49
N. 69

Hodges cont.
N. W. 67, 78
Rev. Mr. 52
S. K. 77
Hoffman, Jacob 40
Juliana 40
Hogg, Euclidus 79
Holcombe, Rev. Mr. 6
Holley, James 71
Hollinshead, Martha 41
Holmes, Catharine 30
Elizabeth F. 39
James G. 39
Joseph 65, 79
Rev. Mr. 37, 45, 64
William 19, 83
Hook, Celina 85
Rachel 84
Hooker, Zadock 79
Hope, J. C. 48, 94
John C. 93
Rev. Mr. 48
Hopkins, James 20
John 73
Keziah 14, 20, 40
Mary T. 17, 43
Hora, Wm. 69
Horry, Elias 13, 39
Francis Ann Margaret 65
Margaret H. 13, 39
Hotchkiss, Hezekiah 27
House, Reuben 14, 40
Howard, Ann 24
Brutus 10
John 67
R. 24
Howe, Mary 72
Prof. 72
Rev. Mr. 68, 81
Howell, Charles 41
Elizabeth 3, 4
Jesse M. 66, 81
Martha S. 66, 81
Robert 4
William 4
Hoy, Ann W. 10
Robert 10
Huggins, Col. 29
Solomon 23
Hughes, John 69
Hughson, William E. 71
Huguenin, Julius G. 13
Hunt, Alfred M. 54
William 13
Hunter, Mary 89
Hussey, Mary S. 62
Hutchinson, Elizabeth M. 55
Thomas 32
Hutting, George 79

Ioor, Benjamin Guignard 65,
80
John 15

Ioor cont.
 Nancy 15
 Peter Horry 69
Izard, Walter 43

Jackson, Gen. 30
James, David 61
 Halloway 24
 John M. 89
 R. W. 85
Jamison, Robert 70
Jenks, Mary Ann 80
 Wm. 74
Jennings, C. P. 44
 J. 54
Jerman, James E. 68, 81
Johns, Thomas 79
 Wm. B. 35
Johnson, Adeline J. 82
 Catharine 5
 Charlotte 61
 Imogena 83
 James 87
 John 61
 John R. 78
 Mary Jane 87
 Rev. Mr. 55
 Richard M. 82, 83
 Samuel 5
 W. B. 67, 78
Johnston, Burr 54
 Harriett Rebecca 54
 Penelope 30
 Richard 7
Joiner, Rev. Mr. 80
Jones, Calvin 25
 Caroline Ann 57
 Conald B. 57
 Donald B. 12
 Emmiline A. 56
 George 63
 Hannah 73
 James 14, 40
 Jonathan 60
 Louise Elonor 63
 Margaret Ann 59, 94
 Mathias 44
 Paul 88
 R. H. 73
 Samuel 73
 Sarah Louise 91
 Temperance 25
 Wm. 25
Jordan, Joseph 53
Jourdan, Uriah 65

Kaigler, George 19, 79
 Maria 19
Keenan, Rowland 15
Kegne, Peter 73
Keith, James C. 18, 43
Kelly, David 12
 Louisa 56, 85

Kennedy, Francis L. 95
 George 15, 26
 Hannah 14
 Isaac 74
 J. C. 48
 John 14
 John A. 57
 John H. 90
 John Henry 74
 Mary Ann 67
 Mary S. 26
 Rev. 19, 58, 59
 Sarah 74
Kennerly, Amelia 11
 David 5
 Eliza Ann 19
 James C. 14, 40
 Joseph 11
 Rachel C. 29
Keeney, J. C. 53, 56
Kersh, Mary Ann 80
Kesler, Mrs. _____ 41
Kew, Daniel H. 50
Kilgore, James 35
 Josiah 20
Kimble, Rebecca 49
Kincaid, James 4
 Nancy 4
King, Benjamin S. 52
 John Jr. 67
 Mitchell 77
 Rufus 14
Kinsler, Ellen 60
 Harmon 23
 John 60
 John L. 55
 Mary 55
Klapman, Hart 16
Knight, George 61
 Sidney Ann 61
Knighter, Nancy 84
Knighton, Nancy 65
Knox, Lucretia 83
 John 48, 49
Koester, Charles Wm. 7
Kougler, Jacob 30

Lafargue, John 11
Landrum, Mr. 70
 Saml. 74
Lane, Ira 9
 Martha E. 54
Laurens, Edward Rutledge
 13, 39
 Eleanor 13, 40
 Henry 13, 40
Lauderdale, Thomas 45
Laval, Jacint 56, 78, 85
 Jacintha 56, 85
 Leonora 78
 Louise Hannah 18
 Sophia 35
Lazarus, Catherine 44

Lazarus cont.
   Henry 44
Leapheart, Jacob 58, 90
Leavens, Helen N. 95
   Joshua 95
Leckie, James T. 20
Ledbetter, Rev. Mr. 70
   Thomas 49
Lee, John W. 47
   Josephine 55
   Mary 36
Leland, A. 60
   A. W. 56
   Rev. Dr. 54, 84(2), 85, 86,
     91(2)
Le Mercier, Rev. Mr. 9
Lester, Harriet Caroline 94
Lettsom, John Coakley 30
Levering, Jesse 83
   Olivia H. P. 83
Levy, Lewis 57, 89
Lewers, Thomas 12
Lewis, Wm. 48, 49
   Wm. L. 58
Ley, Martha 76
Lide, Margaret 75
Lightner, Elizabeth 94
   George 26, 94
Ligon, Thomas 38
Liles, Aromanus 3
Lipscomb, John 12
   Sarah G. 12
Livingston, John S. 70
   Mary R. 49
Lofton, John 14, 40
Logan, John 13, 39
   Susan W. 13, 39
Long, Benjamin 9, 11
   William Henry 9
Longinotti, Jacob 55, 72
   Robetha 55
Loomis, Adin Lawrence 19
Lovelace, Sophia 48
Lovely, Mary 19
Lowndes, Harriet L. 67
   Thomas 67
Lowry, James 27
   John 90
   Thomas 27
   Wm. 27
Lucas, Ann 30
Lumpkin, Peter 6
   Thos. 48
Lunsford, Rebecca 6
   S. 4
Lykes, Jesse 86
Lyle, Rev. Mr. 71
Lyles, Ann 26
   Nathan 51
   Susanna 5
Lyons, George L. 78
   Isaac 19, 59
   Isabella 19

Lyons cont.
   Theodore H. 59

M'Alilley, Samuel 64
M'Call, Capt. 59
M'Cauley, William 17
M'Clintock, Joseph 69
M'Clure, James 54, 70
   Martha 54
M'Collough, Mary 41
   Thomas 41
M'Creary, Harriet 70
   Saml. 70
   Samuel Jr. 38
M'Crory, John 56, 85
   Susanna 56, 85
M'Cullough, Dan'l. 56, 85
   Eliza 35
   James 35
   Robert 39
M'Dowell, Alexander 71, 84
   Nancy 46
M'Duffie, George 77
   Mary Rebecca 77
M'Elroy, M. 46
M'Farland, Neil L. 37
M'Fie, James 58
M'Gee, Rich'd. 30
M'Gill, Susan 33
   Wm. 79
M'Ginny, Elizabeth C. 10
M'Gowen, James 12
M'Guire, Rebecca 53
M'Henry, Mrs. 16
M'Ilvaine, Rev. Mr. 80
M'Ilwain, William 30
M'Kenna, Ann 44
   Wm. 44
M'Kennie, Catharine 67
M'Lean, Neal 23
M'Lelland, George K. D. 94
M'Lemore, Eliza 38
   John 38
M'Millan, Ann Becket 87(2)
   James B. 91
   John 87(2)
   Mary 87(2)
M'Mullan, Jas. C. 70
M'Namara, B. S. 14
   Patrick 34
M'Pherson, Isaac 29(2), 33
   Rev. Mr. 95
M'Queen, Donald 92

McCants, John L. 92
McCary, Benjamin 68
McCaule, Laird Harris 4
   Thomas Harris 4
McCauley, William 42
McCaw, Mrs. 59
McCluney, William 51
McCully, J. B. 60
   Samuel S. 94

McDowell, Alexander 49(2)
   John 96
   Mary 49
   Susannah 96
McDuffie, George 45, 62
   Mary Rebecca 62
McElroy, Wm. 93
McFarland, Duncan 32
   Mary 32
McGarity, Harriet 60
McGowan, Ann 21
   Henry 5
McIver, John 49
McKibben, John 2
   Nancy 2
McKennis, Rev. Mr. 20
McKiernan, Owen 60
McLauchlin, Benjamin 50
McLean, Eliza 50
   Hugh 50
McLemore, Francis Lucinda 70
   Joel 60, 70
   John 60
   Sally 3
McMillan, James B. 91
   Jane A. 70
   Mary 45
   William 91
McMorris, John 53
McMullen, Joseph 52, 82
McNair, Evander 91
McNeal, Augustus 20
McNeille, George 61
   Margaret K. 61
McPherson, M. 54, 59
   Malcom 96
McQueen, Archibald 50
McWhorter, Andrew 42
   Mary Ann D. 42

Mac Fie, James 92
Mac Iver, John 63
Macole, Caledonia C. 20
Madison, Eleanor 23
   George 33
   James 23
Maguire, Peter 55
Mallard, Rev. Mr. 12(2)
Mallary, Rev. Mr. 41
Mallory, R. C. 17
   Rev. Mr. 14, 40, 42
Mandell, Daniel 66, 81
Manley, Joseph 9
Manning, Laurence 9
Marbury, Ellen 23
   William 23
Marbut, Kisiah 79
   Mary 79
   Sarah 79
Marcher, Rev. Mr. 23
Marion, Francis 66
   Gen. 66
Marks, Elias 15, 41, 70

Marks cont.
   Isaac N. 55
   Jane 15, 41
Marsh, Mrs. 32
Marshall, John 73
   William 30
Martin, Caroline 48
   Elizabeth 95
   James 4, 78
   Martha 65, 81
   Rev. Mr. 59
Mason, Benjamin 22
   John 55
   Stephen Thomas 6
Matheson, Farquhar 55
Mathieu, Angelina C. 66, 81
Matthews, Mary 31
Matthias, Barbary 94
Maulding, Millicent F. 65
Maybin, Henry 65, 84
Mayrant, James 94
   John 88, 95
   Margaret 94
   Robert Pringle 65
   William 25
Mays, Caroline E. 68, 81
   Nancy 44
   Richard 78
   Samuel 12, 30, 44
   Samuel W. 73
Maxcy, Esek. H. 17, 42
   Rev. Dr. 11, 33
Maxwell, Mary B. 47
Meacham, Angelina 56
   Dr. 54, 56
   James 61
Means, John 48
   Polly 3
   Rev. Mr. 45, 48
   Rev. R. 50
   Robert 66, 67, 75, 81
   W. B. 66, 81
Meetze, Felix 22
   Rev. Mr. 80
   Spartha 96
Mellard, James H. 57
Meng, Clough S. 41
Meyers, David 76
   Frederick 53
Mickle, John 71
   Joseph 57, 90
   Martha B. 57, 90
Mickler, Andrew 31
Middlemore, W. 30
Middleton, John 96
Miles, James 2
   James S. 88
   Nancy Mibben 2
Miller, Charles W. 82
   Cynthia 70
   Elizabeth 9
   Gov. 46
   William 13, 40

Milling, David 75
    Elizabeth 45
    Hugh 45, 59, 67, 92
    Isabella 67
    Jane 75
    Robert 22
Mills, Dr. 73
    Elanor 71
    Sarah 79
    Wm. 71
Milton, Isham 68
Miott, Charles H. 86
    Ellen 86
Mitchell, Rev. Mr. 59, 94
    Sarah 86
    Thomas R. 91
    Wm. C. 86
Mittag, John F. G. 44
Mobley, Elizabeth 41
    James 41
    John 53
    John Jr. 85
    Mary 41
    Nancy 53
Moffatt, Samuel 40, 73
Mollan, James 13, 40
    Stuart 13
Monroe, James 69
Monteith, Galloway 62
    Mary 92
    Nathaniel 94
Montgomery, Charles 24
    Hugh 79
    Margaret 24
    Rev. Dr. 31
Mood, Rev. Mr. 60
Moore, Alexander 56
    Caroline 58, 91
    Eliza M. 71
    Henrietta 86
    Henry 71
    John D. 22, 46
    John P. 29
    John W. 86
    John Walter 58, 91
    Mary Catherine Ann 46
    Michael 6
    William 58, 69, 86, 91, 95
    William Preston 22
    Wilson A. 58
Moorman, Mary 79
Mooty, Alex. 65
Montgomery, William 6
Mordecai, Benjamin 60
    M. C. 19
Morel, Henrietta 6
    John 6
Morgan, Isaac C. 59
    Joseph H. 55
    Rev. Mr. 36
Morison, Spencer 59, 95
Morris, Gov. 33
    Jordon 90

Morse, John K. 57
Moseley, Mason 11
Moss, Mary E. 73
    Stephen 73
Mott, Rev. M. 78
Muldrow, Harriet A. 85
    Matthew 85
Mulholland, Charles 9
Mullion, Mourning 41
Murdock, Mrs. 14, 40
Murphy, C. T. 54
    John H. 33
    Peter 16
    Thomas F. 43
Murrowe, Rev. Mr. 43, 44
Murtishaw, George B. 67
    Samuel 60
Musco, Mr. 39
Muse, Thomas 21
Myers, David 26, 61, 68, 81
    Conrod 17
    Elizabeth 68, 81
    John J. 60
    Mary 26
    William 38
    William Robert 60

Nagle, Amelia S. 68, 81
    Augustus G. 68, 81
Nance, Laura 89
Neil, John 95
Nelson, James 79
    John 31, 54
Nesbit, John 45
Neuffer, C. 55
    Sarah Caroline 55
Newberry, Rev. Mr. 56
Newbold, John 80
Newell, Henry 91
Newton, Lucy 80
Nicholson, John D. 67
Nickols, Rev. Mr. 84
Nipper, Mary 88
Nixon, John 34
    Wm. 34
Noble, Nathaniel G. 68, 81
Nones, Abraham B. 56
Norane, Joshua P. 44
Norman, Christiana 54
North, Lord 1
Nott, Abraham 61, 76
    Judge 14
Nunamaker, David 80
    G. B. 84
Nutting, George 79
    Jane Ann 72
    Mary 79
    Samuel 85

Oadel, Thomas 47
Oatts, Michael 93
O'Connor, William 89
O'Donovan, Michael 34

O'Farrel, Rev. Mr. 3
O'Farrell, James 31
Odum, Elizabeth 24
Ogletree, Rev. B. 94
O'Hanlon, Ann Matilda 96
  James 68, 81
  T. 96
Oliver, Jane A. 61
  Matthew Howell 72
O'Neal, Richard 80
O'Neil, Rev. Dr. 72
O'Neill, Rev. J. F. 72
Osborn, W. C. 77
Owen, Martha 13
  T. F. 13
Owens, James T. 67

Paccotti, Rackaline 25
Pagand, John 37
Palmer, E. G. 60, 96
  Rev. Mr. 10
Pardue, Morris 2
Park, Amasa T. 61
  Angelina 61
  A. T. 56
  Mary C. 20
  Thomas 20, 56
Parker, Edward F. 64
  Nelly 6
  Thomas 6
Parr, Caroline Harriet 52
  John 31, 52
Parrish, Augustus 58
Parrot, Nancy 16, 42
  Thomas 16, 42
  W. 36
Parsons, Jas. 89
Patrick, Thomas 3
Patterson, Elizabeth 7
  Warren 31
  William 7, 11
Paulding, Rev. M. 41, 68, 81
  Wm. 81
Paulling, W. 13, 40
Pearson, Edward 12
  Gracey 80
  Isaac 35
  Joel E. 45
  Mary 35
  Mary Ann 30
  Mary Rebecca 45
  Philip 32, 83
  Robert R. 32
  Wm. 31
Peay, A. F. 65, 79
  J. E. 45
  Martha K. 65, 79
Peixotta, Rev. Mr. 19
Pelton, Charles B. 54
Pense, Daniel 83
Peoples, Darling 25
Perry, Stuart 55
Petrie, G. H. W. 91

Phillips, Nancy A. 75
Pickens, Israel 15
Picket, Elizabeth 65
  Emelia 49
  Jephthah 39
  John B. 49
  Nancy 39
Pickett, Elizabeth 84
Pierce, James W. 50
Plant, B. D. 19
Player, Col. 72
  George C. 44
  Joshua 51
  Mary 72
Poag, John 70
  Rebecca 95
  William 95
Poindexter, Thomas B. 62
  Thomas K. 48
Polock, Clara 60
  Eliza 57, 89
  Jacabit 76
  L. 57, 60, 89
  Levy 76
Ponsonby, Thomas A. 21
Poole, Eugenia E. 56
  William 72
Pope, Harriet 52
Porlier, Gen. 30
Porter, Jane 26
  John 69
Pou, Ann C. 55
  Joseph 43
Powers, Michael 68
  Susannah 7
Poznanski, Gustavus 60
Pratt, Thomas 12, 91
Pressley, Samuel E. 88
Pressly, Saml. P. 44, 47
Preston, Francis 57
  John 75
  Margaret 57
  Maria 44
  Robert T. 48
  Wm. C. 44, 62, 77
Price, Louisa M. 85
Prince, Lawrence 91
  Mary J. 91
Pringle, John Julius 67
  Mrs. 67
Pritchard, William H. 50
Pullig, Anthony 22
Purvis, Burridge 33
  Robert 71
  William 39
Putman, Elizabeth 81
Pyatt, Joseph 26

Quattlebaum, Capt. 86
  Daniel 48
Quattlebom, Polly 50
Quilter, Thomas 66, 69

Rabb, Mary 33
Ragin, Richard 95
    Sarah A. 95
Rall, Celia 96
    Jacob 96
    Mr. _____ 86
    T. 55
    Thomas 48
Rambert, Caroline 80
Ramsay, Ephraim 50
    James 13, 40
    John 21, 43
    Mary Ann 50
Randolph, John 63
Raney, Rev. M. 21
Raoul, Caroline 61
    John Louisa 42
Ratcliffe, Mary 72
    Norborn 72
    Thomas Campbell 72
    William Preston 72
Rawls, John I. 17
    John J. 42
    Thos. 56, 57
Ray, Rev. Mr. 39
    Thomas 78, 82
Raynal, Marie Martha 50
Rearden, Emeline 67
Reeder, William C. 60
Rees, Maria 86
    Sophia 93
    William 5
    Wm. J. 86
Reese, Mary 95
Reid, Ann T. K. 37
    John 22, 30
    Nancy 34
    Rev. Mr. 12, 31
    Thomas 70
Rembert, Caroline 68
Rene, Rev. Mr. 18
Reney, Rev. Mr. 18(2)
Rennie, Rev. Mr. 16, 23
Resselaeh, K. Van. 33
Reynolds, Jas. H. 81
    J. L. 91
    Rev. Mr. 60, 61, 90
    Thomas G. 38
Rice, Benj. H. 82
    Caroline 83
    David J. 88
    Mary 73
    Sarah P. 73
    Wm. 59, 73, 83, 88
Richards, Benjamin W. 80
Richardson, Elizabeth 92
    James 28
    James M. 52
    Maynard D. 73
    William G. 92
Ricks, Robert G. 48
Riddle, Honirous 80
Ried, George B. 43

Ripley, Ann C. 20
    L. 20, 76
    Mary 7
Rish, John 86
Roberts, John M. 24
Robertson, George 89
Robeson, John W. 17, 43
Robinson, David 95
    E. L. 95
Robison, George 24
Robson, John 38
Rockwell, E. F. 61
Rodes, L. Judge 94
Rogers, Benjamin 89
    James 6, 62, 77, 78
    Jane Wilson 6
    John 16, 42
    Martha Fullerton 16, 42
    Rev. Mr. 30
Root, Francis 60, 90
    Maria 90
    Mary Elizabeth 60
Ross, Rev. Mr. 71
    Thomas 1
Roul, George D. 27
    Mary 27
Rouse, Wm. 24
Rowe, John 8
Rudulph, Michael J. 33
Ruff, Elizabeth 94
    Jno. Henry 64
Rumph, Mary Elvira 12
Russel, Rev. Mr. 41
Russell, Alfred 88
Rutherford, Thomas B. 44
Rutledge, John 27
Ryan, John 17, 43
Ryson, Wright C. 32

Salley, Ann 37
Sally, Jno. J. 73
Sams, H. M. 94
Sancry, Polly 7
Saylor, Caroline 13, 40
    Esais 85
    Mary 31
    Sarah 85
Scraife, Charner T. 60
    Susan Eliza 60
Schenk, Catharine Ann 22
Schrock, David 31
Schutt, Ann 13
Schulz, John C. 9
Schwartz, John G. 69
Scott, Adeline J. 82
    John 41
    John A. 75
    Martha S. 17, 42
    Mary E. 78
    Rev. Mr. 26
    Samuel 24
    Tamer 79
    Thomas W. 82

Scriven, Rev. Mr. 89
Scriver, Rev. Mr. 57
  Wm. 57
Seaborn, Maj. 93
Seibels, Charlotte Caroline 6
  Henry 65
  Jacob 6
  Sarah 59, 65
  William 59
Senn, Conrad 85
  David 89
Service, J. H. 17
Sewell, Rev. J. 83
Seybt, Augustine Eugenia 92
  Frederick 71
  Jane 42
Shackleford, Clara Elizabeth 15
  Francis R. 15
Shand, P. J. 56, 84(2)
  Rev. Mr. 60, 92
  Robert 83
Shands, Rev. Mr. 94
Shannon, Jeremiah 32
Sharp, Joshua 33
  Robert Durham Allen 79
Shaw, James 8
Shell, James 32
  Thomas 31
Shelton, Clough 67
Sheppard, Louisa 14, 40
  Polly 10
Sherman, Levi 73
Shinnie, Alex 53
Shiver, Wm. 89
Shoppert, Precious 31
Sides, Catharine 25
Sill, Edward 15, 41
Simkins, Eldred 73, 76
  Eldred Jr. 73
Simons, Eloiza Hayne 87
  Kealing Lewis 27
  Thomas H. 87
Sims, Ann 92
  David W. 21
  Matthew 42
  Susanna 10
Sindleton, Richard 62
Singleton, Mary Rebecca 45
  Richard 45, 77, 82
  T. D. 50
  Videau Marion 82
Skrine, Susan Mason 8
Slaughter, Gabriel 33
Sligh, John 94
Sloan, Robert 96
Smart, William 3, 26
Smiley, John 12
Smith, Asa T. 21
  Catherine B. 14, 40
  Edward Darell 27
  Eliza 15, 43
  George E. 88
  Henry G. 24

Smith cont.
  I. 32
  J. M'D. 90
  Josiah E. 56
  J. Pearson 83
  Mrs. 1
  Robert M. 51
  Stephen H. 65
  Whiteford 87
  William 1
  W. R. 51
Smoke, Rev. Mr. 65
Smyth, Leslie 96
Snowden, Eliza Jane 15
  Gilbert T. 15
  G. T. 13
Soloman, Mark 93
  Soloman 57
Sondley, Narcissa 49
  Richard 49, 83
Spain, Hartwell 54
Spann, Caroline Margaret 59
  Catherine F. 11
  Charles 59, 89
  Eliza L. 47
  James 89
  Maria L. A. 89
  Richard R. 47
Spencer, Eliza S. 78
  Joel 25
  Samuel 89
  Shepherd 78
Spillars, John 79
Squier, Caleb 63
Stanford, Richard 30
Stanhope, Samuel 27
Stanley, Martha Maria 52
  Robert 76
Stanton, Rachel 31
Stark, James 38
  Robert 38, 77
  Sarah 48
Starke, Mary 26
  Robert 26
  Thomas 11
Steadman, Edward 60
Steele, Jno. B. 52
  Wm. B. 75
Stevens, J. H. 8
Stewart, Adam 87(2)
Stinson, D. J. 94
  Lucretia
Stokes, Rev. Mr. 15(2)
Stone, Emma 76
  Harriet 71
Straud, John 82
Strobel, W. D. 80
Strong, Christopher 86
Strother, John D. 52
Sturtevant, Edwin 85
Suber, Christian 94
  Mary 63
Sullivan, Dunklin 59

Summers, Jesse 58
Sumter, Gen. 73
Sweeny, C. 15, 41
    Catharine 87
    Catharine Rebecca 87
    D. E. 15, 41
    Doyle E. 87
    Napoleon B. 15, 41

Tait, William 11
Talmage, Rev. Mr. 14, 40
Tambaugh, S. C. 25
Tarrant, Benjamin 25
    Sarah 25
Tart, Enos 23
Taylor, Benjamin 51
    Eliza Jane 18
    Elizabeth W. 56
    Gov. 14
    H. 92
    Harriet C. 14, 40
    Henry P. 56, 72
    Jane B. 84
    Jesse 4
    John 30, 62
    John Chestnut 62
    Jonathan 57
    Lavinia 14, 40
    Leah 57
    Mary 4
    Mrs. 51
    R. A. 20
    Samuel 26
    Samuel S. 18
    Samuel W. 90
    Thomas 46, 51
    Thomas F. 46
    William 14, 20, 40
    William H. 18
Telford, William 53
Terondet, Daniel 2
Terrel, John 54
    Sarah A. 54
Terrentine, Rev. Mr. 73
Thigpen, Rev. Mr. 11
Thomas, James 9
Thompson, Charles 53
    Christopher 4
    G. M. 92
    Jno. 53
    Judge 31
    Maria S. 31
    Martha 70
    William 76
Thornton, William 31
Threewitts, Elizabeth Julia 67
    Lewellen 3
Thurman, John 21
Tidwell, Gneuman 19
Tiller, Mary 16
Tillery, Mary 50
Tillinghast, Amy 4
    Daniel H. 29, 33

Tillinghast cont.
    Frances W. 33
    Henry H. 2, 4
    Sally 7
Todd, R. M. 26, 70, 72
Toland, Margaret A. 91
Tompkins, Stephen 73
Toney, Eliza Emily 48
    Jane Caroline 48
    Mary H. 35
    William 48
    Wm. 48
Townes, Samuel 36
Townsend, Rev. Mr. 64
Trap, Sarah 26
Tradewell, Benjamin 13(2),
    52(2), 56, 62, 85
    James D. 73
    Rev. B. 69
    Rev. Mr. 16, 19, 40(2),
        41, 42, 53, 55, 65,
        75, 76
Trantham, Betsy 64
Treadwell, Benjamin 14
    Rev. B. 67
Trezevant, Judge 6
Trimble, Wm. H. 92
Troublefield, Elizabeth 23
Troutman, Hiram B. 25
Tucker, George 63
    John 7
    Thomas Tudor 20
Turner, Joseph 32
    Mrs. 32
Tutt, Elizabeth 36
    Richard 36

Vandever, George 29
Van Lew, George C. 37
Van Rensselaeh, K. 33
Vanuxem, Lardner 80
Veal, John 26
    Mr. 39
    Rebecca 26

Waddell, Esther 96
    Jane E. 58
    Robert 96
    W. W. 75
Waddle, Sarah Ann 52
Wade, George 4, 29,
    Martha 29
    Rebecca 4
    Thomas 4
Wadlington, Dorothy R. 49
Wakely, David L. 68
Walker, Elizabeth 27
    Freeman 17
    Levi 95
    Mary Hoey 60
    R. B. 37
    Robert B. 12
    Tandy 35

Wall, James W. 65, 84
  Wm. 48
Wallace, Caroline Elizabeth 82
  Elizabeth 39
  Elvira 55
  John 55
  W. 82
  William 86
Walsh, John 13
  John G. 46
  Rev. Dr. 26
Ward. H. D. A. 14
Ware, Sarah 25
  Thomas C. 84
Waring, Ann 25
  Benjamin 25, 32
  John M. 84
  Lucy R. 84
Warne, Julia Pierpont 70
Waters, Nicholson 8
Waties, Elizabeth 50
  Judge 50
  Thomas 21
  Wilson 36
Watson, Cloe 69
  Elijah 69
  Sophia 69
  Stanmore 55
  Susanna 49

Watt, Jane 93
  John 93
  Nancy 93
  Thomas 91, 95
Watts, Jonathan 58
Waul, Thomas 18
Wayne, Anthony 3
Weatherall, John 34
Weathers, Thos. J. 81
Weir, Mary 89
Wells, Eliza A. 53
  Dr. 17, 43
  John 5
  Thomas 53
Welsh, Elizabeth 66
Werts, Eliza M. 90
Wessinger, Mathias 31
West, Rev. Dr. 7
  Wm. 37
Weston, Ann 45
  Robert Jr. 47
Wethers, Thomas J. 65
Wheeler, Simeon 21
Whipple, Pardon M. 41
White, Daniel D. 23
  Eleanor N. 14, 40
  Eliza Margaret 88
  Elizabeth 76
  Everett 64
  James J. B. 16, 23, 68, 81
  Jane 90
  Joseph B. 88
  Mary E. 68, 81

White cont.
  Rupert B. 72
  Thomas 14
  William 90
  Willis 14, 40
Whitecotton, Jane E. 90
Whitlow, James M. 37
Wielder, Ann 25
Wilder, Theresa C. 89
  T. J. 89
Wilkins, Samuel B. 36
Willey, Carolina 83
  E. F. 83
  Newton 83
Williams, A. B. 91
  Charlotte J. 81
  David 9
  David R. 63
  Dr. 78
  Eliza A. 78
  Elizabeth 9
  George 71
  Joseph 11
  Mary Ann 55, 75
  Washington 72
  Wm. 25
Williamson, James E. 19
  Mary 2, 17
  Nancy 5
  Rollen 2
  Samuel T. 54
  Thos. 53
  Thomas T. 25
Willingham, John D. 55
Wilson, James 9, 58
  James H. 44
  Mary Caroline 84
  Mrs. James 58
  Peggy 9
  Samuel 22, 84
  William 1, 37
  W. S. 42
Winans, John C. 67
Wingard, Jacob 79
Winn, Benjamin F. 74
  Eliza 1
  Gen. 86
  John Jr. 1
  Peggy 4
  Richard 4
Wise, Anna Barbara 90
  George 90
Witherspoon, J. D. 37
  J. H. 59
  Rev. Dr. 55
Witten, Peter 3
Wolfe, Mary C. 18
Wood, James 70
Woods, James F. 64
Woodward, Cynthia 48
  John 45
  Sarah 24, 61, 76
  Thomas A. 61, 76

113

Woodward cont.
   Wm. T. 34
Wooten, Eliza 65
   Mark 72
Wrench, John T. 77
   Martha A. 50
Wrenchy, John T. 62
Wright, Austin R. 28
Wych, Anne 51
   John 5
Wylie, Alexander 30, 32

Yancey, John 32, 34
   Mary W. 34
Yarborough, Deborah Anne 23
   Washington 23
Yates, Robert 9, 54
   William B. 83
Yeaman, Mary Ann 21
Yeamans, George 18
Yongue, Jemima 16
   J. L. 85
   Nancy 85
   Rachel 12
   Samuel W. 16, 41
Young, Charles 81
   Rebecca 81
   Rev. Mr. 17
Younginer, Elizabeth 57

Zeigler, Mr. 20
Zimmerman, Mary E. 62